healing hearts

*h*ealing
*h*earts

Compassionate Writers

on Breaking Up

EDITED BY JOHN MILLER AND AARON KENEDI

WILLIAM MORROW AND COMPANY, INC.
NEW YORK

Copyright ©2000 by John Miller and Aaron Kenedi

All rights reserved. No part of this book may be reproduced or utilized in any form or by any means, electronic or mechanical, including photocopying, recording, or by any information storage or retrieval system, without permission in writing from the Publisher. Inquiries should be addressed to Permissions Department, William Morrow and Company, Inc., 1350 Avenue of the Americas, New York, N.Y. 10019.

It is the policy of William Morrow and Company Inc., and its imprints and affiliates recognizing the importance of preserving what has been written, to print the books we publish on acid-free paper, and we exert our best efforts to that end.

Library of Congress Cataloging-in-Publication Data
Healing hearts : compassionate writing on breaking up /
edited by John Miller and Aaron Kenedi.
p. cm.
ISBN: 0-688-17274-1
1. Love--Miscellanea. 2. Man-woman relationships--Miscellanea.
3. Separation (Psychology)--Miscellanea. 4. Loss (Psychology)--Miscellanea.
I. Miller, John, 1959- II. Kenedi, Aaron.

BF575.L8 H374 2000
306.73--dc21   99-049324

Printed in the United States of America
First Edition
1 2 3 4 5 6 7 8 9 10
www.williammorrow.com

SPECIAL THANKS TO:

KIM INDRESANO
STEPHANIE HEALD
AMY RENNERT
BESSIE WEISS

contents

THE WEIGHT OF LOSS

Raymond Carver *Blackbird Pie* **11**

Jeanette Winterson *Written on the Body* **41**

Anne Sexton *For My Lover, Returning to His Wife* **45**

Ivan Klima *Divorce* **48**

F. Scott Fitzgerald *The Sensible Thing* **60**

ON THE PATH

Rumi *The Guest House* **84**

M. Scott Peck *The Risk of Loss* **86**

Bernhard Schlink *The Reader* **91**

Alice Adams *His Women* **97**

Laotzu *Tao Te Ching* **99**

A NEW STRENGTH

Denise Chávez *The Wedding* **102**

Rainer Maria Rilke *Letters on Love* **121**

Ovid *The Omen* **125**

W. S. Merwin *The Different Stars* **127**

Maya Angelou *Gather Together in My Name* **130**

ABOUT THE AUTHORS 141

ACKNOWLEDGMENTS 143

the weight of loss

Blackbird Pie

RAYMOND CARVER

I was in my room one night when I heard something in the corridor. I looked up from my work and saw an envelope slide under the door. It was a thick envelope, but not so thick it couldn't be pushed under the door. My name was written on the envelope, and what was inside purported to be a letter from my wife. I say "purported" because even though the grievances could only have come from someone who'd spent twenty-three years observing me on an intimate, day-to-day basis, the charges were outrageous and completely out of keeping with my wife's character. Most important, however, the handwriting was not my wife's handwriting. But if it wasn't her handwriting, then whose was it?

I wish now I'd kept the letter, so I could reproduce it down to the last comma, the last uncharitable exclamation point. The tone is what I'm talking about now, not just the content. But I didn't keep it, I'm sorry to say. I lost it, or else misplaced it.

Later, after the sorry business I'm about to relate, I was cleaning out my desk and may have accidentally thrown it away—which is uncharacteristic of *me*, since I usually don't throw anything away.

In any case, I have a good memory. I can recall every word of what I read. My memory is such that I used to win prizes in school because of my ability to remember names and dates, inventions, battles, treaties, alliances, and the like. I always scored highest on factual tests, and in later years, in the "real world," as it's called, my memory stood me in good stead. For instance, if I were asked right now to give the details of the Council of Trent or the Treaty of Utrecht, or to talk about Carthage, that city razed by the Romans after Hannibal's defeat (the Roman soldiers plowed salt into the ground so that Carthage could never be called Carthage again), I could do so. If called upon to talk about the Seven Years' War, the Thirty Years', or the Hundred Years' War, or simply the First Silesian War, I could hold forth with the greatest enthusiasm and confidence. Ask me anything about the Tartars, the Renaissance popes, or the rise and fall of the Ottoman Empire. Thermopylae, Shiloh, or the Maxim gun. Easy. Tannenberg?

Simple as blackbird pie. The famous four and twenty that were set before the king. At Agincourt, English longbows carried the day. And here's something else. Everyone has heard of the Battle of Lepanto, the last great sea battle fought in ships powered by galley slaves. This fracas took place in 1571 in the eastern Mediterranean, when the combined naval forces of the Christian nations of Europe turned back the Arab hordes under the infamous Ali Muezzin Zade, a man who was fond of personally cutting off the noses of his prisoners before calling in the executioners. But does anyone remember that Cervantes was involved in this affair and had his left hand lopped off in the battle? Something else. The combined French and Russian losses in one day at Borodino were seventy-five thousand men—the equivalent in fatalities of a fully loaded jumbo jet crashing every three minutes from breakfast to sundown. Kutuzov pulled his forces back toward Moscow. Napoleon drew breath, marshalled his troops, and continued his advance. He entered the downtown area of Moscow, where he stayed for a month waiting for Kutuzov who never showed his face again: The Russian generalisimo was waiting for snow and ice, for Napoleon to begin his retreat to France.

Things stick in my head. I remember. So when I say I can re-create the letter—the portion that I read, which catalogues the charges against me—I mean what I say.

In part, the letter went as follows:

Dear,

Things are not good. Things, in fact, are bad. Things have gone from bad to worse. And you know what I'm talking about. We've come to the end of the line. It's over with us. Still, I find myself wishing we could have talked about it.

It's been such a long time now since we've talked. I mean really *talked*. Even after we were married we used to talk and talk, exchanging news and ideas. When the children were little, or even after they were more grownup, we still found time to talk. It was more difficult then, naturally, but we managed, we found time. We *made* time. We'd have to wait until after they were asleep, or else when they were playing outside, or with a sitter. But we managed. Sometimes we'd engage a sitter just so we *could* talk. On occasion we talked the night away, talked until the sun came up. Well. Things happen, I know. Things change. Jack had that trouble with the police, and Linda found herself pregnant, etc. Our quiet time together flew out the window. And gradually your responsibilities backed up on you. Your work became more important, and our time together was squeezed out. Then, once the children left home, our time for talking was back. We had each other again, only we had less and less to talk about. "It happens," I can hear some wise man saying. And he's right. *It happens.* But it happened to us. In any case, no blame. *No blame.* That's not what this letter is about. *I want to talk about us.* I want to talk about *now.* The time has come, you see, to admit that *the impossible* has happened. To cry *Uncle.* To beg off. To—

I read this far and stopped. Something was wrong. Something was fishy in Denmark. The sentiments expressed in the letter may have belonged to my wife. (Maybe they did. Say they did, grant that the sentiments expressed *were* hers.) But the handwriting *was not her handwriting.* And I ought to know. I consider myself an expert in this matter of her handwriting. And yet if it wasn't her handwriting, who on earth *had* written these lines?

I should say a little something about ourselves and our life here. During the time I'm writing about we were living in a house we'd taken for the summer. I'd just recovered from an illness that had set me back in most things I'd hoped to accomplish that spring. We were surrounded on three sides by meadows, birch woods, and some low, rolling hills—a "territorial view," as the realtor had called it when he described it to us over the phone. In front of the house was a lawn that had grown shaggy, owing to lack of interest on my part, and a long gravelled drive that led to the road. Behind the road we could see the distant peaks of mountains. Thus the phrase "territorial view"—having to do with a vista appreciated only at a distance.

My wife had no friends here in the country, and no one came to visit. Frankly, I was glad for the solitude. But she was a woman who was used to having friends, used to dealing with shopkeepers and tradesmen. Out here, it was just the two of us, thrown back on our resources. Once upon a time a house in the country would have been our ideal—we would have *coveted* such an arrangement. Now I can see it wasn't such a good idea. No, it wasn't.

Both our children had left home long ago. Now and then a letter came from one of them. And once in a blue moon, on a holiday, say, one of them might telephone—a collect call, naturally, my wife being only too happy to accept the charges. This seeming indifference on their part was, I believe, a major cause of my wife's sadness and general discontent—a discontent, I have to admit, I'd been vaguely aware of before our move to the country. In any case, to find herself in the country after so many years of living close to a shopping mall and bus service, with a taxi no farther away than the telephone in the hall—it must have been hard on her, very hard. I think her *decline*, as a historian might put it, was accelerated by our move to the country. I think she slipped a cog after that. I'm speaking from hindsight, of course, which always tends to confirm the obvious.

I don't know what else to say in regard to this matter of the handwriting. How much more can I say and still retain credibility? We were alone in the house. No one else—to my knowledge, anyway—was in the house and could have penned the letter. Yet I remain convinced to this day that it was not her handwriting that covered the pages of the letter. After all, I'd been reading my wife's handwriting since before she was my wife. As far back as what might be called our pre-history days—the time she went away to school as a girl, wearing a gray-and-white school uniform. She wrote letters to me every day that she was away, and she was away for two years, not counting holidays and summer vacations. Altogether, in the course of our relationship, I would estimate (a conservative estimate, too), counting our separations and the short periods of time I was away on business or in the hospital, etc.— I would estimate, as I say, that I received seventeen hundred or possibly eighteen hundred and fifty handwritten letters from her, not to mention hundreds, maybe thousands, more informal notes ("On your way home, please pick up dry cleaning, and some spinach pasta from Corti Bros"). I could recognize her handwriting anywhere in the world. Give me a few words. I'm confident that if I were in Jaffa, or Marrakesh, and picked up a note in the marketplace, I would recognize it if it was my wife's handwriting. A word, even. Take this word *"talked,"* for instance. That simply isn't the way she'd write "talked"! Yet I'm the first to admit I don't know *whose* handwriting it is if it isn't hers.

Secondly, my wife *never* underlined her words for emphasis. Never. I don't recall a single instance of her doing this—not once in our entire married life, not to mention the letters I received from her before we were married. It would be reasonable enough, I suppose, to point out that it could happen to anyone. That is, anyone could find himself in a situation that is completely atypical and, *given the pressure of the moment*, do something totally out of character and draw a line, the merest *line*, under a word, or maybe under an entire sentence.

I would go so far as to say that every word of this entire letter, so-called (though I haven't read it through in its entirety, and won't, since I can't find it now), is utterly false. I don't mean false in the sense of "untrue," necessarily. There is some truth, perhaps, to the charges. I don't want to quibble. I don't want to appear small in this matter; things are bad enough already in this department. No. What I want to say, all I want to say, is that while the sentiments expressed in the letter may be my wife's, may even hold *some* truth—be legitimate, so to speak—the force of the accusations levelled against me is diminished, if not entirely undermined, even discredited, because she *did not* in fact write the letter. Or, if she *did* write it, then discredited by the fact that she didn't write it in her own handwriting! Such evasion is what makes men hunger for facts. As always, there are some.

On the evening in question, we ate dinner rather silently but not unpleasantly, as was our custom. From time to time I looked up and smiled across the table as a way of showing my gratitude for the delicious meal—poached salmon, fresh asparagus, rice pilaf with almonds. The radio played softly in the other room; it was a little suite by Poulenc that I'd first heard on a digital recording five years before in an apartment on Van Ness, in San Francisco, during a thunderstorm.

When we'd finished eating, and after we'd had our coffee and dessert, my wife said something that startled me. "Are you planning to be in your room this evening?" she said.

"I am," I said. "What did you have in mind?"

"I simply wanted to know." She picked up her cup and drank some coffee. But she avoided looking at me, even though I tried to catch her eye.

Are you planning to be in your room this evening? Such a question was altogether out of character for her. I wonder now why on earth I didn't pursue this at the time. She knows my habits, if anyone does. But I think her mind was made up even then. I think she was concealing something even as she spoke.

"Of course I'll be in my room this evening," I repeated,

perhaps a trifle impatiently. She didn't say anything else, and neither did I. I drank the last of my coffee and cleared my throat.

She glanced up and held my eyes a moment. Then she nodded, as if we had agreed on something. (But we hadn't, of course.) She got up and began to clear the table.

I felt as if dinner had somehow ended on an unsatisfactory note. Something else—a few words maybe—was needed to round things off and put the situation right again.

"There's a fog coming in," I said.

"Is there? I hadn't noticed," she said.

She wiped away a place on the window over the sink with a dish towel and looked out. For a minute she didn't say anything. Then she said—again mysteriously, or so it seems to me now—"There is. Yes, it's very foggy. It's a heavy fog, isn't it?" That's all she said. Then she lowered her eyes and began to wash the dishes.

I sat at the table a while longer before I said, "I think I'll go to my room now."

She took her hands out of the water and rested them together against the counter. I thought she might proffer a word or two of encouragement for the work I was engaged in, but she didn't. Not a peep. It was as if she were waiting for me to leave the kitchen so she could enjoy her privacy.

Remember, I was at work in my room at the time the letter was slipped under the door. I read enough to question the handwriting and to wonder how it was that my wife had presumably been busy somewhere in the house and writing me a letter at the same time. Before reading further in the letter, I got up and went over to the door, unlocked it, and checked the corridor.

It was dark at this end of the house. But when I cautiously put my head out I could see light from the living room at the end of the hallway. The radio was playing quietly, as usual. Why did I hesitate? Except for the fog, it was a night very much like any other we had spent together in the house. But there was *something else afoot* tonight. At that moment I found myself afraid—afraid, if you can believe it, in my own house!—to walk down the hall and satisfy myself that all was well. Or if something was wrong, if my wife was experiencing—how should I put it?—difficulties of any sort, hadn't I best confront the situation before letting it go any further, before losing any more time on this stupid business of reading her words in somebody else's handwriting!

But I didn't investigate. Perhaps I wanted to avoid a frontal attack. In any case, I drew back and shut and locked the door before returning to the letter. But I was angry now as I saw the evening sliding away in this foolish and incomprehensible business. I was beginning to feel uneasy. (No other word will do.) I could feel my gorge rising as I picked up the letter purporting to be from my wife and once more began to read.

> The time has come and gone for us—us, you and me—to put all our cards on the table. Thee and me. Lancelot and Guinevere. Abélard and Héloïse. Troilus and Cressida. Pyramus and Thisbe. JAJ and Nora Barnacle, etc. You know what I'm saying, honey. We've been together a long time—thick and thin, illness and health, stomach distress, eye-ear-nose-and-throat trouble, high times and low. Now? Well, I don't know what I can say now except the truth: I can't go it another step.

At this point, I threw down the letter and went to the door again, deciding to settle this once and for all. I wanted an accounting, and I wanted it now. I was, I think, *in a rage*. But at this point, just as I opened the door, I heard a low murmuring from the living room. It was as if somebody were trying to say something over the phone and this somebody was taking pains not to be overheard. Then I heard the receiver being replaced. Just this. Then everything was *as before*—the radio playing softly, the house otherwise quiet. But I had heard a voice.

In place of anger, I began to feel panic. I grew afraid as I looked down the corridor. Things were the same as before—the light was on in the living room, the radio played softly. I took a few steps and listened. I hoped I might hear the comforting, rhythmic clicking of her knitting needles, or the sound of a page being turned, but there was nothing of the sort. I took a few steps toward the living room and then—what should I say?—I lost my nerve, or maybe my curiosity. It was at that moment I heard *the muted sound of a doorknob being turned*, and afterward the unmistakable sound of a door opening and closing quietly.

My impulse was to walk rapidly down the corridor and into the living room and get to the bottom of this thing once and for all. But I didn't want to act impulsively and possibly discredit myself. I'm not impulsive, so I waited. But there *was* activity of some sort in the house—something was afoot, I was sure of it—and of course it was my duty, for my own peace of mind, not to mention the possible safety and well-being of my wife, to act. But I didn't. I couldn't. The moment was there, but I hesitated. Suddenly it was too late for any decisive action. The moment had come and gone, and could not be called back. Just so did Darius hesitate and then fail to act at the Battle of Granicus, and the day was lost, Alexander the Great rolling him up on every side and giving him a real walloping.

I went back to my room and closed the door. But *my heart was racing*. I sat in my chair and, trembling, picked up the pages of the letter once more.

But now here's the curious thing. Instead of beginning to read the letter through, from start to finish, or even starting at the point where I'd stopped earlier, I took pages at random and held them under the table lamp, picking out a line here and a line there. This allowed me to juxtapose the charges made against me until the entire indictment (for that's what it was) took on quite another character—one more acceptable, since it had lost its chronology and, with it, a little of its punch.

So. Well. In this manner, going from page to page, here a line, there a line, I read in snatches the following—which might under different circumstances serve as a kind of abstract:

> . . . withdrawing farther into. . . a small enough thing, but . . . talcum powder sprayed over the bathroom, including walls and baseboards . . . a shell . . . not to mention the insane asylum . . . until finally . . . a balanced view . . . the grave. Your "work" . . . Please! Give me a break . . . No one, not even . . . Not another word on the subject! . . . The children . . . but the real issue . . . not to mention the loneliness . . . Jesus H. Christ! Really! I mean . . .

At this point I distinctly heard the front door close. I dropped the pages of the letter onto the desk and hurried to the living room. It didn't take long to see that my wife wasn't in the house. (The house is small—two bedrooms, one of which we refer to as my room or, on occasion, as my study.) But let the record show: *every light in the house was burning.*

A heavy fog lay outside the windows, a fog so dense I could scarcely see the driveway. The porch light was on and a suitcase stood outside on the porch. It was my wife's suitcase, the one she'd brought packed full of her things when we moved here. What on earth was going on? I opened the door. Suddenly—I don't know how to say this other than how it was—a horse stepped out of the fog, and then, an instant later, as I watched, dumfounded, another horse. These horses were grazing in our front yard. I saw my wife alongside one of the horses, and I called her name.

"Come on out here," she said. "Look at this. Doesn't this beat anything?"

She was standing beside this big horse, patting its flank. She was dressed in her best clothes and had on heels and was wearing a hat. (I hadn't seen her in a hat since her mother's funeral, three years before.)

"Where did you come from, you big baby?" she said. "Where did you come from, sweetheart?" Then, as I watched, she began to cry into the horse's mane.

"There, there," I said and started down the steps. I went over and patted the horse, and then I touched my wife's shoulder. She drew back. The horse snorted, raised its head a moment, and then went to cropping the grass once more.

"What is it?" I said to my wife. "For God's sake, what's happening here, anyway?"

She didn't answer. The horse moved a few steps but continued pulling and eating the grass. The other horse was munching grass as well. My wife moved with the horse, hanging on to its mane. I put my hand against the horse's neck and felt a surge of power run up my arm to the shoulder. I shivered. My wife was still crying. I felt helpless, but I was scared, too.

"Can you tell me what's going on?" I said. "Why are you dressed like this? What's the suitcase doing on the front porch? Where did these horses come from? For God's sake, can you tell me what's happening?"

My wife began to croon to the horse. Croon! Then she stopped and said, "You didn't read my letter, did you? You might have skimmed it, but you didn't read it. Admit it!"

"I did read it," I said. I was lying, yes, but it was a white lie. A partial untruth. But he who is blameless, let him throw out the first stone. "But tell me what is going on anyway," I said.

My wife turned her head from side to side. She pushed her face into the horse's dark wet mane. I could hear the horse *chomp, chomp, chomp*. Then it snorted as it took in air through its nostrils.

She said, "There was this girl, you see. Are you listening? And this girl loved this boy so much. She loved him even more than herself. But the boy—well, he grew up. I don't know what happened to him. Something, anyway. He got cruel without meaning to be cruel and he—"

I didn't catch the rest, because then a car appeared out of the fog, in the drive, with its headlights on and a flashing blue light on its roof. It was followed, a minute later, by a pickup truck pulling what looked like a horse trailer, though with the fog it was hard to tell. It could have been anything—a big portable oven, say. The car pulled right up onto the lawn and stopped. Then the pickup drove alongside the car and stopped, too. Both vehicles kept their headlights on and their engines running, which contributed to the eerie, bizarre aspect of things. A man wearing a cowboy hat—a rancher, I supposed— stepped down from the pickup. He raised the collar of his sheepskin coat and whistled to the horses. Then a big man in a raincoat got out of the car. He was a much bigger man than the rancher, and he, too, was wearing a cowboy hat. But his raincoat was open, and I could see a pistol strapped to his waist. He had to be a deputy sheriff. Despite everything that was going on, and the anxiety I felt, I found it *worth noting* that both men were wearing hats. I ran my hand through my hair, and was sorry I wasn't wearing a hat of my own.

"I called the sheriff's department a while ago," my wife said. "When I first saw the horses." She waited a minute and then she said something else. "Now you won't need to give me a ride into town after all. I mentioned that in my letter, the letter you read. I said I'd need a ride into town. I can get a ride—at least, I think I can—with one of these gentlemen. And I'm not changing my mind about anything, either. I'm saying this decision is irrevocable. Look at me!" she said.

I'd been watching them round up the horses. The deputy was holding his flashlight while the rancher walked a horse up a little ramp into the trailer. I turned to look at this woman I didn't know any longer.

"I'm leaving you," she said. "That's what's happening. I'm heading for town tonight. I'm striking out on my own. It's all in the letter you read." Whereas, as I said earlier, my wife never underlined words in her letters for emphasis, she was now speaking (having dried her tears) as if virtually every other word out of her mouth ought to be underlined.

"What's gotten *into* you?" I heard myself say. It was almost as if I couldn't help adding pressure to some of my own words. "Why are you *doing* this?"

She shook her head. The rancher was loading the second horse into the trailer now, whistling sharply, clapping his hands and shouting an occasional "Whoa! Whoa, damn you! Back up now. Back up!"

The deputy came over to us with a clipboard under his arm. He was holding a big flashlight. "Who called?" he said.

"I did," my wife said.

The deputy looked her over for a minute. He flashed the light onto her high heels and then up to her hat. "You're all dressed up," he said.

"I'm leaving my husband," she said.

The deputy nodded, as if he understood. (But he didn't, he couldn't!) "He's not going to give you any trouble, is he?" the deputy said, shining his light into my face and moving the light up and down rapidly. "You're not, are you?"

"No," I said. "No trouble. But I resent—"

"Good," the deputy said. "Enough said, then."

The rancher closed and latched the door to his trailer.

Then he walked toward us through the wet grass, which, I noticed, reached to the tops of his boots.

"I want to thank you folks for calling," he said. "Much obliged. That's one heavy fog. If they'd wandered onto the main road, they could have raised hob out there."

"The lady placed the call," the deputy said. "Frank, she needs a ride into town. She's leaving home. I don't know who the injured party is here, but she's the one leaving." He turned then to my wife. "You sure about this, are you?" he said to her.

She nodded. "I'm sure."

"O.K.," the deputy said. "That's settled, anyway. Frank, you listening? I can't drive her to town. I've got another stop to make. So can you help her out and take her into town? She probably wants to go to the bus station or else to the hotel. That's where they usually go. Is that where you want to go to?" the deputy said to my wife. "Frank needs to know."

"He can drop me off at the bus station," my wife said. "That's my suitcase on the porch."

"What about it, Frank?" the deputy said.

"I guess I can, sure," Frank said, taking off his hat and

putting it back on again. "I'd be glad to, I guess. But I don't want to interfere in anything."

"Not in the least," my wife said. "I don't want to be any trouble, but I'm—well, I'm distressed just now. Yes, I'm distressed. But it'll be all right once I'm away from here. Away from this awful place. I'll just check and make doubly sure I haven't left anything behind. Anything *important*," she added. She hesitated and then she said, "This isn't as sudden as it looks. It's been coming for a long, long time. We've been married for a good many years. Good times and bad, up times and down. We've had them all. But it's time I was on my own. Yes, it's time. Do you know what I'm saying, gentlemen?"

Frank took off his hat again and turned it around in his hands as if examining the brim. Then he put it back on his head.

The deputy said, "These things happen. Lord knows none of us is perfect. We weren't made perfect. The only angels is to be found in Heaven."

My wife moved toward the house, picking her way through the wet, shaggy grass in her high heels. She opened the front door and went inside. I could see her moving behind the lighted windows, and something came to me then. *I might never see her again*. That's what crossed my mind, and it staggered me.

The rancher, the deputy, and I stood around waiting, not saying anything. The damp fog drifted between us and the lights from their vehicles. I could hear the horses shifting in the trailer. We were all uncomfortable, I think. But I'm speaking only for myself, of course. I don't know what they felt. Maybe they saw things like this happen every night—saw people's lives flying apart. The deputy did, maybe. But Frank, the rancher, he kept his eyes lowered. He put his hands in his front pockets and then took them out again. He kicked at something in the grass. I folded my arms and went on standing there, not knowing what was going to happen next. The deputy kept turning off his flashlight and then turning it on again. Every so often he'd reach out and swat the fog with it. One of the horses whinnied from the trailer, and then the other horse whinnied, too.

"A fellow can't see anything in this fog," Frank said.

I knew he was saying it to make conversation.

"It's as bad as I've ever seen it," the deputy said. Then he looked over at me. He didn't shine the light in my eyes this time, but he said something. He said, "Why's she leaving you?

You hit her or something? Give her a smack, did you?"

"I've never hit her," I said. "Not in all the time we've been married. There was reason enough a few times, but I didn't. She hit me once," I said.

"Now, don't get started," the deputy said. "I don't want to hear any crap tonight. Don't say anything, and there won't be anything. No rough stuff. Don't even think it. There isn't going to be any trouble here tonight, is there?"

The deputy and Frank were watching me. I could tell Frank was embarrassed. He took out his makings and began to roll a cigarette.

"No," I said. "No trouble."

My wife came onto the porch and picked up her suitcase. I had the feeling that not only had she taken a last look around but she'd used the opportunity to freshen herself up, put on new lipstick, etc. The deputy held his flashlight for her as she came down the steps. "Right this way, Ma'am," he said. "Watch your step, now—it's slippery."

"I'm ready to go," she said.

"Right," Frank said. "Well, just to make sure we got this all straight now." He took off his hat once more and held it.

"I'll carry you into town and I'll drop you off at the bus station. But, you understand, I don't want to be in the middle of something. You know what I mean." He looked at my wife, and then he looked at me.

"That's right," the deputy said. "You said a mouthful. Statistics show that your domestic dispute is, time and again, potentially the most dangerous situation a person, especially a law-enforcement officer, can get himself involved in. But I think this situation is going to be the shining exception. Right, folks?"

My wife looked at me and said, "I don't think I'll kiss you. No, I won't kiss you goodbye. I'll just say so long. Take care of yourself."

"That's right," the deputy said. "Kissing—who knows what that'll lead to, right?" He laughed.

I had the feeling they were all waiting for me to say something. But for the first time in my life I felt at a loss for words. Then I *took heart* and said to my wife, "The last time you wore that hat, you wore a veil with it and I held your arm. You were in mourning for your mother. And you wore a dark dress, not the dress you're wearing tonight. But those are the same high heels, I remember. Don't leave me like this," I said. "I don't know what I'll do."

"I have to," she said. "It's all in the letter—everything's spelled out in the letter. The rest is in the area of—I don't know. Mystery or speculation, I guess. In any case, there's nothing in the letter you don't already know." Then she turned to Frank and said, "Let's go, Frank. I can call you Frank, can't I?"

"Call him anything you want," the deputy said, "long as you call him in time for supper." He laughed again—a big, hearty laugh.

"Right," Frank said. "Sure you can. Well, O.K. Let's go, then." He took the suitcase from my wife and went over to his pickup and put the suitcase into the cab. Then he stood by the door on the passenger's side, holding it open.

"I'll write after I'm settled," my wife said. "I think I will, anyway. But first things first. We'll have to see."

"Now you're talking," the deputy said. "Keep all lines of communication open. Good luck, pardee," the deputy said to me. Then he went over to his car and got in.

The pickup made a wide, slow turn with the trailer across the lawn. One of the horses whinnied. The last image I have of my wife was when a match flared in the cab of the pickup, and I saw her lean over with a cigarette to accept the light the rancher was offering. Her hands were cupped around the hand that held the match. The deputy waited until the pickup and trailer had gone past him and then he swung his car around, slipping in the wet grass until he found purchase on the driveway, throwing gravel from under his tires. As he headed for the road, he tooted his horn. *Tooted.* Historians should use more words like "tooted" or "beeped" or "blasted"—especially at serious moments such as after a massacre or when an awful occurrence has cast a pall on the future of an entire nation. That's when a word like "tooted" is necessary, is gold in a brass age.

I'd like to say it was at this moment, as I stood in the fog watching her drive off, that I remembered a black-and-white photograph of my wife holding her wedding bouquet. She was eighteen years old—*a mere girl,* her mother had shouted at me only a month before the wedding. A few minutes before the photo, she'd gotten married. She's smiling. She's just finished, or is just about to begin, laughing. In either case, her mouth is open in amazed happiness as she looks into the camera. She is three months pregnant, though the camera doesn't show that, of course. But what if she *is* pregnant? So what? Wasn't everybody pregnant in those days? She's happy, in any case. I was happy, too—I know I was. We were both happy. I'm not in that particular picture, but I was close—only a few steps away, as I remember, shaking hands with someone offering me good wishes. My wife knew Latin and German and chemistry and physics and history and Shakespeare and all those other things they teach you in private school. She knew how to properly hold a teacup. She also knew how to cook and to make love. She was a prize.

But I found this photograph, along with several others, a few days after the horse business, when I was going through my wife's belongings, trying to see what I could throw out and what I should keep. I was packing to move, and I looked at the photograph for a minute and then I threw it away. I was ruthless. I told myself I didn't care. Why should I care?

If I know anything—and I do—if I know the slightest thing about human nature, I know she won't be able to live without me. She'll come back to me. And soon. Let it be soon.

No, I don't know anything about anything, and I never did. She's gone for good. She is. I can feel it. Gone and never coming back. Period. Not ever. I won't see her again, unless we run into each other on the street somewhere.

There's still the question of the handwriting. That's a bewilderment. But the handwriting business isn't the important thing, of course. How could it be after the consequences of the letter? Not the letter itself but the things I can't forget that were *in* the letter. No, the letter is not paramount at all—there's far more to this than somebody's handwriting. The "far more" has to do with subtle things. It could be said, for instance, that to take a wife is to take a history. And if that's so, then I understand that I'm outside history now—like horses and fog. Or you could say that my history has left me. Or that I'm having to go on *without history*. Or that history will now have to do without me—unless my wife writes more letters, or tells a friend who keeps a diary, say. Then, years later, someone can look back on this time, interpret it according to the record, its scraps and tirades, its silence and innuendos. That's when it dawns on me that autobiography is the poor man's history. And that I am saying goodbye to history. Goodbye, my darling.

Written on the Body

JEANETTE WINTERSON

Why is the measure of love loss?

It hasn't rained for three months. The trees are prospecting underground, sending reserves of roots into the dry ground, roots like razors to open any artery water-fat.

The grapes have withered on the vine. What should be plump and firm, resisting the touch to give itself in the mouth, is spongy and blistered. Not this year the pleasure of rolling blue grapes between finger and thumb juicing my palm with musk. Even the wasps avoid the thin brown dribble. Even the wasps this year. It was not always so.

I am thinking of a certain September: Wood pigeon Red Admiral Yellow Harvest Orange Night. You said, 'I love you.' Why is it that the most unoriginal thing we can say to one another is still the thing we long to hear? 'I love you' is always a quotation. You did not say it first and neither did I, yet when you say it and when I say it we speak like savages who have found three words and worship them. I did worship them but now I am alone on a rock hewn out of my own body.

CALIBAN   You taught me language and my profit on it is
                I know how to curse. The red plague rid you
                For learning me your language.

Love demands expression. It will not stay still, stay silent, be good, be modest, be seen and not heard, no. It will break out in tongues of praise, the high note that smashes the glass and spills the liquid. It is no conservationist love. It is a big game hunter and you are the game. A curse on this game. How can you stick at a game when the rules keep changing? I shall call myself Alice and play croquet with the flamingos. In Wonderland everyone cheats and love is Wonderland isn't it? Love makes the world go round. Love is blind. All you need is love. Nobody ever died of a broken heart. You'll get over it. It'll be different when we're married. Think of the children. Time's a great healer. Still waiting for Mr. Right? Miss Right? and maybe all the little Rights?

It's the cliches that cause the trouble. A precise emotion seeks a precise expression. If what I feel is not precise then should I call it love? It is so terrifying, love, that all I can do is shove it under a dump bin of pink cuddly toys and send myself a greetings card saying 'Congratulations on your Engagement'. But I am not engaged I am deeply distracted. I am desperately looking the other way so that love won't see me. I want the diluted version, the sloppy language, the insignificant gestures. The saggy armchair of cliches. It's all right, millions of bottoms have sat here before me. The springs are well worn, the fabric smelly and familiar. I don't have to be frightened, look, my grandma and grandad did it, he in a stiff collar and club tie, she in white muslin straining a little at the life beneath. They did it, my parents did it, now I will do it won't I, arms outstretched, not to hold you, just to keep my balance, sleepwalking to that armchair. How happy we will be. How happy everyone will be. And they all lived happily ever after.

We lay on our bed in the rented room and I fed you plums the colour of bruises. Nature is fecund but fickle. One year she leaves you to starve, the next year she kills you with love. That year the branches were torn beneath the weight, this year they sing in the wind. There are no ripe plums in August.

Have I got it wrong, this hesitant chronology? Perhaps I should call it Emma Bovary's eyes or Jane Eyre's dress. I don't know. I'm in another rented room now trying to find the place to go back to where things went wrong. Where I went wrong. You were driving but I was lost in my own navigation.

Nevertheless I will push on. There were plums and I broke them over you.

You said, 'Why do I frighten you?'

Frighten me? Yes you do frighten me. You act as though we will be together for ever. You act as though there is infinite pleasure and time without end. How can I know that? My experience has been that time always ends. In theory you are right, the quantum physicists are right, the romantics and the religious are right. Time without end. In practice we both wear a watch. If I rush at this relationship it's because I fear for it. I fear you have a door I cannot see and that any minute now the door will open and you'll be gone. Then what? Then what as I bang the walls like the Inquisition searching for a saint? Where will I find the secret passage? For me it'll just be the same four walls.

For My Lover, Returning to His Wife

ANNE SEXTON

She is all there.
She was melted carefully down for you
and cast up from your childhood,
cast up from your one hundred favorite aggies.

She has always been there, my darling.
She is, in fact, exquisite.
Fireworks in the dull middle of February
and as real as a cast-iron pot.

Let's face it, I have been momentary.
A luxury. A bright red sloop in the harbor.
My hair rising like smoke from the car window.
Littleneck clams out of season.

She is more than that. She is your have to have,
has grown you your practical your tropical growth.

HEALING HEARTS

This is not an experiment. She is all harmony.
She sees to oars and oarlocks for the dinghy,

has placed wild flowers at the window at breakfast,
sat by the potter's wheel at midday,
set forth three children under the moon,
three cherubs drawn by Michelangelo,

done this with her legs spread out
in the terrible months in the chapel.
If you glance up, the children are there
like delicate balloons resting on the ceiling.

she has also carried each one down the hall
after supper, their heads privately bent,
two legs protesting, person to person,
her face flushed with a song and their little sleep.

I give you back your heart.
I give you permission—

for the fuse inside her, throbbing
angrily in the dirt, for the bitch in her
and the burying of her wound—
for the burying of her small red wound alive–

for the pale flickering flare under her ribs,
for the drunken sailor who waits in her left pulse,
for the mother's knee, for the stockings,
for the garter belt, for the call—

the curious call
when you will burrow in arms and breasts
and tug at the orange ribbon in her hair
and answer the call, the curious call.

She is so naked and singular.
She is the sum of yourself and your dream.
Climb her like a monument, step after step.
She is solid.

As for me, I am a watercolor.
I wash off.

Divorce

IVAN KLIMA

It was true that Judge Martin Vacek had dealt with a number of political cases under the old regime, but, as he was only five years away from retirement age, it was suggested that from now on he should deal exclusively with divorce cases (which, in any event, is what he had done when he first came to the bench). He considered this to be an acceptable, even sensible, proposal. He could, of course, have left the bench altogether, as several of his colleagues had, and set up privately as a barrister, which was far more lucrative. But he was conservative by nature and had no wish to alter his daily routine or his regular journey to work, let alone start looking for and equipping private offices. Nonetheless, he consulted his wife about what he should do.

He had been married for thirty years and had stopped loving his wife, Marie, long ago; in fact, he could no longer remember a time when he actually loved her. Nevertheless, they got on fairly well together. His wife, who was a year older than he, came from the country and had only an elementary schooling; she had spent her life working at the post office for paltry wages. She did, however, have a natural wisdom, unspoiled by legal training. Marie had plainly stopped loving him years ago, too, but she looked after him almost like a mother, cooking him good meals and making sure that his shirts were ironed and that he always had a suitable tie to wear with them. In the course of their life together, she was bound to have influenced if not his character then at least his appearance, and since they both favored the color gray their very features gradually began to take on a gray cast, too.

In recent years, each had come to regard the other as an indispensable part of the household, particularly now that their two sons had grown up and moved away and the apartment felt empty, although it was crammed with all sorts of useless objects and knick-knacks. They barely spoke anymore, but there had been a time when they went out together to the cinema or to concerts (it was the done thing for someone in his position to have a season ticket for the Philharmonic), or Marie would tell him about the novels she was reading. Nowadays, though, they simply exchanged a few words about food, shopping, their sons, or the weather, or else they watched television together in silence. It therefore came as a surprise to Marie when he asked her whether he should remain on the bench or start something entirely new. It was not her custom to contradict her husband, and in the past when he had asked her opinion, she had always tried to guess the reply he wanted to hear. "Divorce suits," she now said. "That could be fairly interesting work. You'll get to hear lots of stories."

It had never occurred to him to view his possible future employment from such an angle. He had heard so many stories in his lifetime that they had long since ceased to engage him. Nonetheless, he took his wife's opinion into account and remained on the bench.

As it turned out, the cases tended to be more banal than interesting. In most of them, immature men had married young women who yearned for something that their husbands could not provide, and so in time a third person came along who disrupted what had never been firmly established in the first place. Even so, his rulings—on grounds of infidelity or mutual incompatibility—were often met with tears, and Martin could never rid himself of the conviction that most of the divorces were unnecessary, that people were attempting to escape the inescapable: their own emptiness, their own incapacity to share their lives with another person.

There were so many cases that they soon became indistinguishable, and even the people's faces slipped quickly from his memory—which was beginning to decline with age anyway. Now and then, however, an intriguing case would crop up, and a face, a name, or an occupation would stick in his mind.

After one such sitting, he emerged from the courtroom and found the woman to whom he had just given a divorce sitting on a bench in the corridor, crying. The woman's name was Lída Vachková, a name that had caught his eye because of its resemblance to his own, quite apart from the fact that the woman's distinctive, delicate beauty and her timid replies to his questions in court had held his attention. He attributed her delicacy to her profession; she was violinist. Although it was uncharacteristic of him, he stopped in front of her and said, "Don't cry, Mrs. Vachková. No pain lasts forever."

She glanced up at him in surprise and quickly wiped away her tears. "Thank you."

As she got up, she started to sway and he was obliged to catch hold of her. "Are you feeling unwell?"

"Do forgive me," she said. "I took some tablets this morning. To calm my nerves."

He invited her into his chambers and got her a glass of water. He knew not only her name and occupation but also her age. She was twenty years his junior, very young, in his eyes, at least. He also had met the man who until a short while ago had been her husband. The husband, too, was older than she was (although at this moment Martin couldn't recall exactly how much older) and ran some recently established entertainment agency. A vulgar, unpleasant-looking fellow, he had apparently subjected his wife to rough and domineering treatment and had tried to curb all her enthusiasms. There were no children. They had had no problem agreeing on the division of their property—there wasn't very much anyway. She kept the apartment and he moved in with his mistress.

"Do you really believe no pain lasts forever?" she asked.

"Of course."

"Did you ever have a pain that went away?"

He was not accustomed to being cross-examined and was taken aback. He had to stop and think for a moment whether anything in his life had caused him a pain that had later gone away. On the contrary, things in life had tended to fade gradually, without hurt. Then he recalled the death of his parents. "Even the pain of death eventually goes away," he said evasively.

"That true," she conceded. "Though death is a rather special category."

"What makes you think so?"

"Death is like the law. There is no escape from it. Whereas love. . . ." She seemed to be searching for a word to express the meaning of love, but instead burst into tears once again.

He helped her to her feet and saw her to the door and down the stairs. He then suggested they go to a nearby wine bar. He wasn't sure why he was behaving in this way. There must be something about this young woman that touched him, or perhaps it was that he found her attractive. He ordered a bottle of wine and let the woman speak about her recent tribulations, although he took in only a few details; he was gazing at her hands, her fingers involuntarily toying with the napkin. They were so beautiful that he wanted to clasp them in his and stroke them. From time to time he would interrupt her and tell her some of the incidents he had heard about in the course of his work, to reassure her that she was far from alone in her suffering.

When they parted, an hour later, she invited him to a concert to be performed by the orchestra she played in. She also, naturally, invited his wife, but in the end he went alone. He found it impossible to concentrate on the music; his attention was focussed on her single form in the orchestra—the flickering movements of her fingers and her fine bowing—and he felt an unwonted emotion. He was astounded at himself and at his feelings, which struck him as inappropriate for someone his age. But then it occurred to him that he had simply written off certain emotions too soon.

He found her address and telephone number in the case file.

They started to meet twice a week, initially in a café or a wine bar. He was aware that because of his profession she regarded him as an expert in matters of love, or rather on those instances where love was foundering, and indeed when questioned he sought to draw more general lessons from the cases that lay in his memory. Even though he had little belief in the possibility of people living together in love, he realized how cautious he was in his comments, and how he could speak about something he had been unable to achieve in his own life: a relationship of mutual admiration and respect out of which tenderness grew. She listened to him with an increasing hopefulness. "I expect you're good at love," she said and gave his hand a momentary squeeze. "You strike me as someone who can be tolerant and allow the other person some space for herself."

He nodded, pleased that she should think of him in that way.

Then she invited him home.

She lived in a tiny attic room, and as he walked up the many stairs (the house had no elevator) his legs were buckling under him from excitement or maybe anxiety at what was certainly about to happen.

The little room had sloping walls and almost no furniture, just a wardrobe, a music stand, two chairs, and a large divan beneath a skylight. They made love underneath that window.

She was slim and finely built compared with his wife, and her skin was smooth, without a single fold or wrinkle. To his surprise, he found tender words for her. She listened to him, and he had barely stopped speaking when she said, "More, please. I want more of those words." As he was leaving, she asked, "Will we see each other again sometime?" And he assured her that he would certainly be back soon.

And so he would visit her, bringing her flowers, wine, and words of tenderness. They never spoke about her former husband, and he mentioned his wife only occasionally, and always in a way that let Lída assume that his marriage was not particularly happy. As usually happens when information comes from one side only, she would have concluded, had she made the effort, that the fault lay with his wife.

On one occasion, when they were again lying beneath the skylight, onto which the heavy drops of a spring downpour were falling, she asked him, "Do you love your wife at all?"

He said he didn't, that he hadn't loved her for many years.

Then for a long time neither of them said anything. She cuddled up to him as he stroked her hips and her belly, the softness of her skin exciting him as always.

"What's the point of such a marriage, Martin?" she asked abruptly.

The question caught him unprepared. He had never considered the possibility that he might leave his wife after thirty years of living with her, not even now, as he lay at the side of a woman he had just made love to. He had long ceased wondering what bound him to his wife. Habit, perhaps. So many shared days and nights. Memories that now felt like stories about someone else. Maybe the chairs they sat on, or the familiar odor that wafted toward him the moment he opened the door of their apartment. Maybe the sons they had reared.

"You don't have to tell me if you don't want to," she said.

"Maybe," he said, "so that when I come home in weather like this I can say to someone, 'It's raining out.'"

"Yes, that's a good reason," she said, drawing away from him slightly.

As he was leaving, she didn't ask, as she usually did, when they would see each other again. So he asked instead.

"Maybe never," she said. Even so, she leaned toward him and kissed him.

On his way downstairs, it occurred to him that she had been expecting a different response, that he had mistaken the meaning of her question. She had wanted to hear whether he was prepared to leave his wife for her.

He was overcome by an almost weary dejection. He could still turn back, ring her doorbell, and give her a different answer. But what answer should he give?

So Judge Martin Vacek went home.

When he opened the door of his apartment, the familiar odor wafted toward him. Marie came out of the living room and greeted him as usual with the words "I'll have your dinner ready straightaway."

He sat down at the table and stared silently ahead of him. He saw nothing. On the radio in the adjoining room someone was playing the violin. He found the sound of it so distressing that he could hardly move. His wife placed a bowl of hot soup in front of him.

He knew he ought to say something, but he had only an emptiness that engulfed all speech. "It's raining out," he said eventually.

His wife looked toward the window in surprise. It had stopped raining long ago, and the room was suffused with the dark-red glow of the setting sun.

It was her custom not to contradict the husband, even though he had seemed to her more and more absent-minded lately; perhaps old age was beginning to affect his mind.

"That's good," she said. "The farmers fields could do with a bit more moisture."

The Sensible Thing

F. SCOTT FITZGERALD

Jonquil Cary was her name, and to George O'Kelly nothing had ever looked so fresh and pale as her face when she saw him and fled to him eagerly along the station platform. Her arms were raised to him, her mouth was half parted for his kiss, when she held him off suddenly and lightly and, with a touch of embarrassment, looked around. Two boys, somewhat younger than George, were standing in the background.

"This is Mr. Craddock and Mr. Holt," she announced cheerfully. "You met them when you were here before."

Disturbed by the transition of a kiss into an introduction and suspecting some hidden significance, George was more confused when he found that the automobile which was to carry them to Jonquil's house belonged to one of the two young men. It seemed to put him at a disadvantage. On the way Jonquil chattered between the front and back seats, and when he tried to slip his arm around her under cover of the twilight she compelled him with a quick movement to take her hand instead.

"Is this street on the way to your house?" he whispered. "I don't recognize it."

"It's the new boulevard. Jerry just got this car today, and he wants to show it to me before he takes us home."

When, after twenty minutes, they were deposited at Jonquil's house, George felt that the first happiness of the meeting, the joy he had recognized so surely in her eyes back in the station, had been dissipated by the intrusion of the ride. Something that he had looked forward to had been rather casually lost, and he was brooding on this as he said good night stiffly to the two young men. Then his ill-humor faded as Jonquil drew him into a familiar embrace under the dim light of the front hall and told him in a dozen ways, of which the best was without words, how she had missed him. Her emotion reassured him, promised his anxious heart that everything would be all right.

They sat together on the sofa, overcome by each other's

presence, beyond all except fragmentary endearments. At the supper hour Jonquil's father and mother appeared and were glad to see George. They liked him, and had been interested in his engineering career when he had first come to Tennessee over a year before. They had been sorry when he had given it up and gone to New York to look for something more immediately profitable, but while they deplored the curtailment of his career they sympathized with him and were ready to recognize the engagement. During dinner they asked about his progress in New York.

"Everything's going fine," he told them with enthusiasm. "I've been promoted—better salary."

He was miserable as he said this—but they were all *so* glad.

"They must like you," said Mrs. Cary, "that's certain—or they wouldn't let you off twice in three weeks to come down here."

"I told them they had to," explained George hastily; "I told them if they didn't I wouldn't work for them any more."

"But you ought to save your money," Mrs. Cary

reproached him gently. "Not spend it all on this expensive trip."

Dinner was over—he and Jonquil were alone and she came back into his arms.

"So glad you're here," she sighed. "Wish you never were going away again, darling."

"Do you miss me?"

"Oh, so much, so much."

"Do you—do other men come to see you often? Like those two kids?"

The question surprised her. The dark velvet eyes stared at him.

"Why, of course they do. All the time. Why—I've told you in letters that they did, dearest."

This was true—when he had first come to the city there had been already a dozen boys around her, responding to her picturesque fragility with adolescent worship, and a few of them perceiving that her beautiful eyes were also sane and kind.

"Do you expect me never to go anywhere"—Jonquil demanded, leaning back against the sofa-pillows until she seemed to look at him from many miles away—"and just fold my hands and sit still—forever?"

"What do you mean?" he blurted out in a panic. "Do you mean you think I'll never have enough money to marry you?"

"Oh, don't jump at conclusions so, George."

"I'm not jumping at conclusions. That's what you said."

George decided suddenly that he was on dangerous grounds. He had not intended to let anything spoil this night. He tried to take her again in his arms, but she resisted unexpectedly, saying:

"It's hot. I'm going to get the electric fan."

When the fan was adjusted they sat down again, but he was in a supersensitive mood and involuntarily he plunged into the specific world he had intended to avoid.

"When will you marry me?"

"Are you ready for me to marry you?"

All at once his nerves gave way, and he sprang to his feet.

"Let's shut off that damned fan," he cried, "it drives me wild. It's like a clock ticking away all the time I'll be with you. I came here to be happy and forget everything about New York and time—"

He sank down on the sofa as suddenly as he had risen. Jonquil turned off the fan, and drawing his head down into her lap began stroking his hair.

"Let's sit like this," she said softly, "just sit quiet like this, and I'll put you to sleep. You're all tired and nervous and your sweetheart'll take care of you."

"But I don't want to sit like this," he complained, jerking up suddenly, "I don't want to sit like this at all. I want you to kiss me. That's the only thing that makes me rest. And anyways I'm not nervous—it's you that's nervous. I'm not nervous at all."

To prove that he wasn't nervous he left the couch and plumped himself into a rocking-chair across the room.

"Just when I'm ready to marry you you write me the most nervous letters, as if you're going to back out, and I have to come rushing down here—"

"You don't have to come if you don't want to."

"But I *do* want to!" insisted George.

It seemed to him that he was being very cool and

logical and that she was putting him deliberately in the wrong. With every word they were drawing farther and farther apart—and he was unable to stop himself or to keep worry and pain out of his voice.

But in a minute Jonquil began to cry sorrowfully and he came back to the sofa and put his arm around her. He was the comforter now, drawing her head close to his shoulder, murmuring old familiar things until she grew calmer and only trembled a little, spasmodically, in his arms. For over an hour they sat there, while the evening pianos thumped their last cadences into the street outside. George did not move, or think, or hope, lulled into numbness by the premonition of disaster. The clock would tick on, past eleven, past twelve, and then Mrs. Cary would call down gently over the banister—beyond that he saw only to-morrow and despair.

In the heat of the next day the breaking-point came. They had each guessed the truth about the other, but of the two she was the more ready to admit the situation.

"There's no use going on," she said miserably, "you know you hate the insurance business, and you'll never do well in it."

"That's not it," he insisted stubbornly; "I hate going on alone. If you'll marry me and come with me and take a chance with me, I can make good at anything, but not while I'm worrying about you down here."

She was silent a long time before she answered, not thinking—for she had seen the end—but only waiting, because she knew that every word would seem more cruel than the last. Finally she spoke:

"George, I love you with all my heart, and I don't see how I can ever love any one else but you. If you'd been ready for me two months ago I'd have married you—now I can't because it doesn't seem to be the sensible thing."

He made wild accusations—there was some one else—she was keeping something from him!

"No, there's no one else."

This was true. But reacting from the strain of this affair she had found relief in the company of young boys like Jerry Holt, who had the merit of meaning absolutely nothing in her life.

George didn't take the situation well, at all. He seized

her in his arms and tried literally to kiss her into marrying him at once. When this failed, he broke into a long monologue of self-pity, and ceased only when he saw that he was making himself despicable in her sight. He threatened to leave when he had no intention of leaving, and refused to go when she told him that, after all, it was best that he should.

For a while she was sorry, then for another while she was merely kind.

"You'd better go now," she cried at last, so loud that Mrs. Cary came down-stairs in alarm.

"Is something the matter?"

"I'm going away, Mrs. Cary," said George brokenly. Jonquil had left the room.

"Don't feel so badly, George." Mrs. Cary blinked at him in helpless sympathy—sorry and, in the same breath, glad that the little tragedy was almost done. "If I were you I'd go home to your mother for a week or so. Perhaps after all this is the sensible thing—"

"Please don't talk," he cried. "Please don't say anything to me now!"

Jonquil came into the room again, her sorrow and her

nervousness alike tucked under powder and rouge and hat.

"I've ordered a taxicab," she said impersonally. "We can drive around until your train leaves."

She walked out on the front porch. George put on his coat and hat and stood for a minute exhausted in the hall—he had eaten scarcely a bite since he had left New York. Mrs. Cary came over, drew his head down and kissed him on the cheek, and he felt very ridiculous and weak in his knowledge that the scene had been ridiculous and weak at the end. If he had only gone the night before—left her for the last time with a decent pride.

The taxi had come, and for an hour these two that had been lovers rode along the less-frequented streets. He held her hand and grew calmer in the sunshine, seeing too late that there had been nothing all along to do or say.

"I'll come back," he told her.

"I know you will," she answered, trying to put a cheery faith into her voice. "And we'll write each other—sometimes."

"No," he said, "we won't write. I couldn't stand that. Some day I'll come back."

"I'll never forget you, George."

They reached the station, and she went with him while he bought his ticket.

"Why, George O'Kelly and Jonquil Cary!"

It was a man and a girl whom George had known when he had worked in town, and Jonquil seemed to greet their presence with relief. For an interminable five minutes they all stood there talking; then the train roared into the station, and with ill-concealed agony in his face George held out his arms toward Jonquil. She took an uncertain step toward him, faltered, and then pressed his hand quickly as if she were taking leave of a chance friend.

"Good-by, George," she was saying, "I hope you have a pleasant trip."

"Good-by, George. Come back and see us all again."

Dumb, almost blind with pain, he seized his suitcase, and in some dazed way got himself aboard the train.

Past clanging street-crossings, gathering speed through wide suburban spaces toward the sunset. Perhaps she too would see the sunset and pause for a moment, turning, remembering, before he faded with her sleep into the past.

This night's dusk would cover up forever the sun and the trees and the flowers and laughter of his young world.

On a damp afternoon in September of the following year a young man with his face burned to a deep copper glow got off a train at a city in Tennessee. He looked around anxiously, and seemed relieved when he found that there was no one in the station to meet him. He taxied to the best hotel in the city where he registered with some satisfaction as George O'Kelly, Cuzco, Peru.

Up in his room he sat for a few minutes at the window looking down into the familiar street below. Then with his hand trembling faintly he took off the telephone receiver and called a number.

"Is Miss Jonquil in?"

"This is she."

"Oh—" His voice after overcoming a faint tendency to waver went on with friendly formality.

"This is George Rollins. Did you get my letter?"

"Yes. I thought you'd be in to-day."

Her voice, cool and unmoved, disturbed him, but not as

he had expected. This was the voice of a stranger, unexcited, pleasantly glad to see him—that was all. He wanted to put down the telephone and catch his breath.

"I haven't seen you for—a long time." He succeeded in making this sound offhand. "Over a year."

He knew how long it had been—to the day.

"It'll be awfully nice to talk to you again."

"I'll be there in about an hour."

He hung up. For four long seasons every minute of his leisure had been crowded with anticipation of this hour, and now this hour was here. He had thought of finding her married, engaged, in love—he had not thought she would be unstirred at his return.

There would never again in his life, he felt, be another ten months like these he had just gone through. He had made an admittedly remarkable showing for a young engineer—stumbled into two unusual opportunities, one in Peru, whence he had just returned, and another, consequent upon it, in New York, whither he was bound. In this short time he had risen from poverty into a position of unlimited opportunity.

He looked at himself in the dressing-table mirror. He was almost black with tan, but it was a romantic black, and in the last week, since he had had time to think about it, it had given him considerable pleasure. The hardiness of his frame, too, he appraised with a sort of fascination. He had lost part of an eyebrow somewhere, and he still wore an elastic bandage on his knee, but he was too young not to realize that on the steamer many women had looked at him with unusual tributary interest.

His clothes, of course, were frightful. They had been made for him by a Greek tailor in Lima—in two days. He was young enough, too, to have explained this sartorial deficiency to Jonquil in his otherwise laconic note. The only further detail it contained was a request that he should *not* be met the station.

George O'Kelly, of Cuzco, Peru, waited an hour and a half in the hotel, until, to be exact, the sun had reached a midway position in the sky. Then, freshly shaven and talcum-powdered toward a somewhat more Caucasian hue, for vanity at the last minute had overcome romance, he engaged a taxicab and set out for the house he knew so well.

He was breathing hard—he noticed this but he told himself that it was excitement, not emotion. He was here; she was not married—that was enough. He was not even sure what he had to say to her. But this was the moment of his life that he felt he could least easily have dispensed with. There was no triumph, after all, without a girl concerned, and if he did not lay his spoils at her feet he could at least hold them for a passing moment before her eyes.

The house loomed up suddenly beside him, and his first thought was that it had assumed a strange unreality. There was nothing changed—only everything was changed. It was smaller and it seemed shabbier than before—there was no cloud of magic hovering over its roof and issuing from the windows of the upper floor. He rang the door-bell and an unfamiliar colored maid appeared. Miss Jonquil would be down in a moment. He wet his lips nervously and walked into the sitting-room—and the feeling of unreality increased. After all, he saw, this was only a room, and not the enchanted chamber where he had passed those poignant hours. He sat in a chair, amazed to find it a chair, realizing that his imagination had distorted and colored all these simple familiar things.

Then the door opened and Jonquil came into the room—and it was as though everything in it suddenly blurred before his eyes. He had not remembered how beautiful she was, and he felt his face grow pale and his voice diminish to a poor sigh in his throat.

She was dressed in pale green, and a gold ribbon bound back her dark, straight hair like a crown. The familiar velvet eyes caught his as she came through the door, and a spasm of fright went through him at her beauty's power of inflicting pain.

He said "Hello," and they each took a few steps forward and shook hands. Then they sat in chairs quite far apart and gazed at each other across the room.

"You've come back," she said, and he answered just as tritely: "I wanted to stop in and see you as I came through."

He tried to neutralize the tremor in his voice by looking anywhere but at her face. The obligation to speak was on him, but, unless he immediately began to boast, it seemed that there was nothing to say. There had never been anything casual in their previous relations—it didn't seem possible that people in this position would talk about the weather.

"This is ridiculous," he broke out in sudden embarrassment. "I don't know exactly what to do. Does my being here bother you?"

"No." The answer was both reticent and impersonally sad. It depressed him.

"Are you engaged?" he demanded.

"No."

"Are you in love with some one?"

She shook her head.

"Oh." He leaned back in his chair. Another subject seemed exhausted—the interview was not taking the course he had intended.

"Jonquil," he began, this time on a softer key, "after all that's happened between us, I wanted to come back and see you. Whatever I do in the future I'll never love another girl as I've loved you."

This was one of the speeches he had rehearsed. On the steamer it had seemed to have just the right note—a reference to the tenderness he would always feel for her combined with a non-committal attitude toward his present state of mind. Here with the past around him, beside him, growing minute by minute more heavy on the air, it seemed theatrical and stale.

She made no comment, sat without moving, her eyes fixed on him with an expression that might have meant everything or nothing.

"You don't love me any more, do you?" he asked her in a level voice.

"No."

When Mrs. Cary came in a minute later, and spoke to him about his success—there had been a half-column about him in the local paper—he was a mixture of emotions. He knew now that he still wanted this girl, and he knew that the past sometimes comes back—that was all. For the rest he must be strong and watchful and he would see.

"And now," Mrs. Cary was saying, "I want you two to go and see the lady who has the chrysanthemums. She particularly told me she wanted to see you because she'd read about you in the paper."

They went to see the lady with the chrysanthemums. They walked along the street, and he recognized with a sort of excitement just how her shorter footsteps always fell in between his own. The lady turned out to be nice, and the chrysanthemums were enormous and extraordinarily beautiful. The lady's gardens were full of them, white and pink and yellow, so that to be among them was a trip back into the heart of summer. There were two gardens full, and a gate between them; when they strolled toward the second garden the lady went first through the gate.

And then a curious thing happened. George stepped aside to let Jonquil pass, but instead of going through she stood still and stared at him for a minute. It was not so much the look, which was not a smile, as it was the moment of silence. They saw each other's eyes, and both took a short, faintly accelerated breath, and then they went on into the second garden. That was all.

The afternoon waned. They thanked the lady and walked home slowly, thoughtfully, side by side. Through dinner too they were silent. George told Mr. Cary something of what had happened in South America, and managed to let it be known that everything would be plain sailing for him in the future.

Then dinner was over, and he and Jonquil were alone in

the room which had seen the beginning of their love affair and the end. It seemed to him long ago and inexpressibly sad. On that sofa he had felt agony and grief such as he would never feel again. He would never be so weak or so tired and miserable and poor. Yet he knew that that boy of fifteen months before had had something, a trust, a warmth that was gone forever. The sensible thing—they had done the sensible thing. He had traded his first youth for strength and carved success out of despair. But with his youth, life had carried away the freshness of his love.

"You won't marry me, will you?" he said quietly.

Jonquil shook her dark head.

"I'm never going to marry," she answered.

He nodded.

"I'm going on to Washington in the morning," he said.

"Oh—"

"I have to go. I've got to be in New York by the first, and meanwhile I want to stop off in Washington."

"Business!"

"No-o," he said as if reluctantly. "There's some one

there I must see who was very kind to me when I was so—down and out."

This was invented. There was no one in Washington for him to see—but he was watching Jonquil narrowly, and he was sure that she winced a little, that her eyes closed and then opened wide again.

"But before I go I want to tell you the things that happened to me since I saw you, and, as maybe we won't meet again, I wonder if—if just this once you'd sit in my lap like you used to. I wouldn't ask except since there's no one else—yet—perhaps it doesn't matter."

She nodded, and in a moment was sitting in his lap as she had sat so often in that vanished spring. The feel of her head against his shoulder, of her familiar body, sent a shock of emotion over him. His arms holding her had a tendency to tighten around her, so he leaned back and began to talk thoughtfully into the air.

He told her of a despairing two weeks in New York which had terminated with an attractive if not very profitable job in a construction plant in Jersey City. When the Peru business had first presented itself it had not seemed an extraordinary opportunity. He was to be third assistant engineer on the expedition, but only ten of the American party, including eight rodmen and surveyors, had ever reached Cuzco. Ten days later the chief of the expedition was dead of yellow fever. That had been his chance, a chance for anybody but a fool, a marvellous chance—

"A chance for anybody but a fool?" she interrupted innocently.

"Even for a fool," he continued. "It was wonderful. Well, I wired New York—"

"And so," she interrupted again, "they wired that you ought to take a chance?"

"Ought to!" he exclaimed, still leaning back. "That I *had* to. There was no time to lose—"

"Not a minute?"

"Not a minute."

"Not even time for—" she paused.

"For what?"

"Look."

He bent his head forward suddenly, and she drew herself to him in the same moment, her lips half open like a flower.

"Yes," he whispered into her lips. "There's all the time in the world...."

All the time in the world—his life and hers. But for an instant as he kissed her he knew that though he search through eternity he could never recapture those lost April hours. He might press her close now till the muscles knotted on his arms—she was something desirable and rare that he had fought for and made his own—but never again an intangible whisper in the dusk, or on the breeze of night....

Well, let it pass, he thought; April is over, April is over. There are all kinds of love in the world, but never the same love twice.

on the path

The Guest House

RUMI

This being human is a guest house.
Every morning a new arrival.

A joy, a depression, a meanness,
some momentary awareness comes
as an unexpected visitor.

Welcome and entertain them all!
Even if they're a crowd of sorrows,
who violently sweep your house
empty of its furniture,
still, treat each guest honorably.
He may be clearing you out
for some new delight.

The dark thought, the shame, the malice,
meet them at the door laughing,
and invite them in.

Be grateful for whoever comes,
because each has been sent
as a guide from beyond.

The Risk of Loss

M. SCOTT PECK

The act of love—extending oneself—as I have said, requires a moving out against the inertia of laziness (work) or the resistance engendered by fear (courage). Let us turn now from the work of love to the courage of love. When we extend ourselves, our self enters new and unfamiliar territory, so to speak. Our self becomes a new and different self. We do things we are not accustomed to do. We change. The experience of change, of unaccustomed activity, of being on unfamiliar ground, of doing things differently is frightening. It always was and always will be. People handle their fear of change in different ways, but the fear is inescapable if they are in fact to change. Courage is not the absence of fear; it is the making of action in spite of fear, the moving out against the resistance engendered by fear into the unknown and into the future. On some level spiritual growth, and therefore love, always requires courage and involves risk. It is the risking of love that we will now consider.

If you are a regular churchgoer you might notice a woman in her late forties who every Sunday exactly five minutes before the start of the service inconspicuously takes the same seat in a side pew on the aisle at the very back of the church. The moment the service is over she quietly but quickly makes for the door and is gone before any of the other parishioners and before the minister can come out onto the steps to meet with his flock. Should you manage to accost her—which is unlikely—and invite her to the coffee social hour following the service, she would thank you politely, nervously looking away from you, but tell you that she has a pressing engagement, and would then dash away. Were you to follow her toward her pressing engagement you would find that she returns directly to her home, a little apartment where the blinds are always drawn, unlocks her door, enters, immediately locks the door behind her, and is not seen again that Sunday. If you could keep watch over her you might see that she has a job as a low ranking typist in a large office, where she accepts her assignments wordlessly, types them faultlessly, and returns her finished work without comment. She eats her lunch at her desk and has no friends. She walks home, stopping always at the same impersonal supermarket for a few provisions before she vanishes behind her door until she appears again for the next day's work. On Saturday afternoons she goes alone to a local movie theater that has a weekly change of shows. She has a TV set. She has no phone. She almost never receives mail. Were you somehow able to communicate with her and comment that her life seemed lonely, she would tell you that she rather enjoyed her loneliness. If you asked her if she didn't even have any pets, she would tell you that she had a dog of whom she was very fond but that he had died eight years before and no other dog could take his place.

Who is this woman? We do not know the secrets of her heart. What we do know is that her whole life is devoted to avoiding risks and that in this endeavor, rather than enlarging her self, she has narrowed and diminished it almost to the point of nonexistence. She cathects no other living thing. Now, we have said that simple cathexis is not love, that love transcends cathexis. This is true, but love requires cathexis for a beginning. We can love only that which in one way or another has importance for us. But with cathexis there is always the risk of loss or rejection. If you move out to another human being, there is always the risk that that person will move away from you, leaving you more painfully alone than you were before. Love anything that lives—a person, a pet, a plant—and it will die. Trust anybody and you may be hurt; depend on anyone and that one may let you down. The price of cathexis is pain. If someone is determined not to risk pain, then such a person must do without many things: having children, getting married, the ecstasy of sex, the hope of ambition, friendship—all that makes life alive, meaningful and significant. Move out or grow in any dimension and pain as well as joy will be your reward. A full life will be full of pain. But the only alternative is not to live fully or not to live at all.

The essence of life is change, a panoply of growth and decay. Elect life and growth, and you elect change and the prospect of death. A likely determinant for the isolated, narrow life of the woman described was an experience or series of experiences with death which she found so painful that she was determined never to experience death again, even at the cost of living. In avoiding the experience of death she had to avoid growth and change. She elected a life of sameness free from the new, the unexpected, a living death, without risk or challenge. I have said that the attempt to avoid legitimate suffering lies at the root of all emotional illness. Not surprisingly, most psychotherapy patients (and probably most nonpatients, since neurosis is the norm rather than the exception) have a problem, whether they are young or old, in facing the reality of death squarely and clearly. What is surprising is that the psychiatric literature is only beginning to examine the significance of this phenomenon. If we can live with the knowledge that death is our constant companion, traveling on our "left shoulder," then death can become in the words of Don Juan, our "ally," still fearsome but continually a source of wise counsel. With death's counsel, the constant awareness of the limit of our time to live and love, we can always be guided to make the best use of our time and live life to the fullest. But if we are unwilling to fully face the fearsome presence of death on our left shoulder, we deprive ourselves of its counsel and cannot possibly live or love with clarity. When we shy away from death, the ever-changing nature of things, we inevitably shy away from life.

The Reader

BERNHARD SCHLINK

Next day she was gone. I came at the usual time and rang the bell. I looked through the door, everything looked the way it always did, I could hear the clock ticking.

I sat down on the stairs once again. During our first few months, I had always known what line she was working on, even though I had never repeated my attempt to accompany her or even pick her up afterwards. At some point I had stopped asking, stopped even wondering. It hadn't even occurred to me until now.

I used the telephone booth at the Wilhelmsplatz to call the streetcar company, was transferred from one person to the next, and finally was told that Hanna Schmitz had not come to work. I went back to Bahnhofstrasse, asked at the carpenter's shop in the yard for the name of the owner of the building, and got a name and address in Kirchheim. I rode over there.

"Frau Schmitz? She moved out this morning."

"And her furniture?"

"It's not her furniture."

"How long did she live in the apartment?"

"What's it to you?" The woman who had been talking to me through a window in the door slammed it shut.

In the administration building of the streetcar company, I talked my way through to the personnel department. The man in charge was friendly and concerned.

"She called this morning early enough for us to arrange for a substitute, and said that she wouldn't be coming back, period." He shook his head. "Two weeks ago she was sitting there in your chair and I offered to have her trained as a driver, and she throws it all away."

It took me some days to think of going to the citizens' registration office. She had informed them she was moving to Hamburg, but without giving an address.

The days went by and I felt sick. I took pains to make sure my parents and my brothers and sisters noticed nothing. I joined in the conversation at table a little, ate a little, and when I had to throw up, I managed to make it to the toilet. I went to school and to the swimming pool. I spent my afternoons there in an out-of-the-way place where no one would look for me. My body yearned for Hanna. But even worse than my physical desire was my sense of guilt. Why hadn't I jumped up immediately when she stood there and run to her! This one moment summed up all my halfheartedness of the past months, which had produced my denial of her, and my betrayal. Leaving was her punishment.

Sometimes I tried to tell myself that it wasn't her I had seen. How could I be sure it was her when I hadn't been able to make out the face? If it had been her, wouldn't I have had to recognize her face? So couldn't I be sure it wasn't her at all?

But I knew it was her. She stood and looked—and it was too late.

After Hanna left the city, it took a while before I stopped watching for her everywhere, before I got used to the fact that afternoons had lost their shape, and before I could look at books and open them without asking myself whether they were suitable for reading aloud. It took a while before my body stopped yearning for hers; sometimes I myself was aware of my arms and legs groping for her in my sleep, and my brother reported more than once at table that I had called out "Hanna" in the night. I can also remember classes at school when I did nothing but dream of her, think of her. The feeling of guilt that had tortured me in the first weeks gradually faded. I avoided her building, took other routes, and six months later my family moved to another part of town. It wasn't that I forgot Hanna. But at a certain point the memory of her stopped accompanying me wherever I went. She stayed behind, the way a city stays behind as a train pulls out of the station. It's there, somewhere behind you, and you could go back and make sure of it. But why should you?

I remember my last years of school and my first years at university as happy. Yet I can't say very much about them. They were effortless; I had no difficulty with my final exams at school or with the legal studies that I chose because I couldn't think of anything else I really wanted to do; I had no difficulty with friendships, with relationships or the end of relationships—I had no difficulty with anything.

Everything was easy; nothing weighed heavily. Perhaps that is why my bundle of memories is so small. Or do I keep it small? I also wonder if my memory of happiness is even true. If I think about it more, plenty of embarrassing and painful situations come to mind, and I know that even if I had said goodbye to my memory of Hanna, I had not overcome it. Never to let myself be humiliated or humiliate myself after Hanna, never to take guilt upon myself or feel guilty, never again to love anyone whom it would hurt to lose—I didn't formulate any of this as I thought back then, but I know that's how I felt.

I adopted a posture of arrogant superiority. I behaved as if nothing could touch or shake or confuse me. I got involved in nothing, and I remember a teacher who saw through this and spoke to me about it; I was arrogantly dismissive. I also remember Sophie. Not long after Hanna left the city, Sophie was diagnosed with tuberculosis. She spent three years in a sanitorium, returning just as I went to university. She felt lonely, and sought out contact with her old friends. It wasn't hard for me to find a way into her heart. After we slept together, she realized I wasn't interested in her; in tears, she asked, "What's happened to you, what's happened to you?" I remember my grandfather during one of my last visits before his death; he wanted to bless me, and I told him I didn't believe in any of that and didn't want it. It is hard for me to imagine that I felt good about behaving like that. I also remember that the smallest gesture of affection would bring a lump to my throat, whether it was directed at me or at someone else. Sometimes all it took was a scene in a movie. This juxtaposition of callousness and extreme sensitivity seemed suspicious even to me.

His Women

ALICE ADAMS

Although he had every reason to know that she was unhappy, Carter was devastated by Isabel's departure. Against all reason, miserably, he felt that his life was demolished. Irrationally, instead of remembering a bitter, complaining Isabel ("I can't stand this tacky town a minute longer") or an Isabel with whom things did not work out well in bed ("Well, Jesus Christ, is that what you learned at The Citadel?"), he recalled only her beauty. Her clothes, and her scents. Her long blond hair.

He was quite surprised, at first, when Meredith began to call a lot with messages of sympathy, when she seemed to take his side. "You poor guy, you certainly didn't deserve this" was one of the things that she said at the time. Told that he was finding it hard to eat—"I don't know, everything I try tastes awful"—she began to arrive every day or so, at mealtimes, with delicately flavored chicken, and oven-fresh

Sally Lunn, tomatoes from her garden, and cookies, lots and lots of homemade cookies. Then she took to inviting him to her house for dinner—often.

As he left her house, at night, Carter would always kiss Meredith, in a friendly way, but somehow, imperceptibly, the kisses and their accompanying embraces became more prolonged. Also, Carter found that his good-night moment was something he looked forward to. Until the night when Meredith whispered to him, "You really don't have to go home, you know. You could stay with me." More kissing, and then, "Please stay. I want you, my darling Carter."

Sex with Meredith was sweet and pleasant and friendly, and if it lacked the wild rush that he had sometimes felt with Isabel, at least when he failed her she was nice about it. Sweet and comforting. Unlike angry Isabel.

Tao Te Ching

LAOTZU

Nonbeing gives birth to the oneness.
The oneness gives birth to yin and yang.
Yin and yang give birth to heaven, earth,
    and beings.
Heaven, earth, and beings give birth to
    everything in existence.

Therefore everything in existence carries
    within it both yin and yang, and attains
    its harmony by blending together
    these two vital breaths.

Ordinary people hate nothing more than to be
    powerless, small, and unworthy.
Yet this is how superior people
    describe themselves.

Gain is loss.
Loss is gain.

I repeat what others have said:
The strong and violent don't die natural deaths.
This is the very essence of my teaching.

a new strength

The Wedding

DENISE CHÁVEZ

If my marriage is going to be like my wedding, then I'm in for a lot of trouble. For one thing, that Saturday there was a tornado watch all day. We never have tornadoes in Agua Oscura. I don't know anyone that's ever seen one either. I can't ask any relatives about it. I don't have any. I didn't even ask my stepbrothers and stepsisters to the wedding, not that they would have come. I don't like them. Now my stepmom, Lucha, she woulda come. My stepdad, Arturo, he mighta come too, except they're both dead. I guess family not being there means they won't get in the way. Not *my* family, anyway. Hector's family might. His mom, Dolly, likes to get in the middle of things, and so does his sister, Soveida. They always have to know what you're doing. They'll settle down. It's the old lady, Lupita, who really worries me. She told me when we were alone that if it weren't for me, Hector could have a future. I told Hector, and he said: "Relax, Mamá's old. She doesn't like that you're pregnant."

"Well, that's just too bad. I am and there's nothing she can do about it, Hector."

"Just relax, babes, she'll chill."

I don't know, she's pretty scary in that way old ladies who don't like you can be scary. And yet, I like her. If I had a grandmother, I'd probably want one just like her. She's kinda short, with a little extra padding so that she hugs solid the way only a woman like that can. I don't know, maybe Mamá will like me someday. Maybe when the baby is born.

But I was telling you about the wedding. When I woke up this morning it was already ten o'clock, and I hadn't done my hair yet. By the time I put in the rinse and curled it, it was noon. I woke up late, because I'd gone out with La Virgie Lozano and some other girlfriends the night before. We drove to El Paso to see a male revue, the Chippendales. They weren't so Chippendale, after all. One of the guys had real skinny legs and another was too hairy. "These aren't no Chippendales," I told La Virgie, "the Chippendales don't have no body hair. Somebody messed up. These guys are from Ysleta or Sunland Park. Somebody just handed them a jock strap and forgot to grease them up."

I took a long time with my hair and then I had to do my nails. I wanted to be sure all the little gold wedding bells were glued on tight on all my fingernails. That took me until one. The wedding was at two o'clock. I was barely in my dress when El Gonie and La Virgie came to get me to take me to the church. I wasn't supposed to see Hector before the wedding. Now that's pretty hard when you're living in the same apartment.

So he spent the night at his mom's. El Gonie says they went out drinking. As for me, I slept the best I've slept in a long time. Not enough. But really good.

Hector promised me he'd have the rings there and to tell you the truth, I was worried. When I walked down the aisle, I didn't know if the rings were going to be there or not. If they weren't, I was gonna kill him.

"You'll have to wait and see them," he said.

"I don't want no Woolworth rings, Hector Dosamantes, you hear me? Nothing cheap with gold that chips off the first sinkful of dishes. Which by the way, we're gonna share. If you expect me to be your slave, you have another thing in your brain. We're gonna share the housework, not like how it's been, me cleaning up after you like I was your mother or something. When we're married, things are going to change."

"Oh yeah?" Hector says. "I suppose you'll lose your interest in sex. That's what El Gonie said happened after his first and second marriages. Soon as they had the papers, Nora Jean and Tancy lost interest. No way I'll support that, Ada," he tells me.

And I tell him: "Don't worry about it so much. I'm pregnant, aren't I? I showed an interest before, so just don't think about it now."

"I got to think about it. That's what marriage is: sexual relations, two bodies melting into one."

"Oh, yeah?" I says. "Well, it's even more than that. It's holding hands and having a family and taking care of each other. I've never had a family of my own, so now I want one."

"Why do you think I'm getting married? To have a son."

"Do we have to call the baby Hector Jr.? That's the stupidest, dumbest name in the whole world."

"It's *my* name."

"That's what I mean."

"Well, if it's a boy we have to call him Hector, Jr."

"And if it's a girl?"

"If it's a girl, which it won't be, I'll figure it out."

I'm hoping the baby's a girl. If it's a boy, well, no way he's going to be called Hector, Jr.

So here I am walking up the aisle, by myself, no one to walk me up. When I get to the front, I trip over Mr. Dosamantes' lap robe. He's in a wheelchair sitting up there on the groom's side, but his blanket is over on the bride's side of the pews. This is Our Lady of Grace Church. The grandmother's idea. I wanted to say our vows in Juárez and spend the night over there at Sylvia's listening to mariachis, but no way.

I nearly trip and I drag the blanket with me as Hector pulls it back. Then El Gonie picks it up. Soveida is out of her pew, and Lupita's maid starts giggling. I get mad, but then Hector looks at me, and I say *Jesus, just settle down*, with my eyes, and I walk up to the altar. The priest is up there. I don't like the way he looks. All skinny and like he's about to tell you how holy he is. He's Filipino or something, and the guy doesn't have a sense of humor. And what's even worse, the priest keeps forgetting my name.

"Do you . . . ah . . . ah . . . take Hector for your lawful, wedded, husband . . . Hector, do you take . . . ah . . . ah . . . ah . . . as your . . . ah . . . lawful wedded wife?"

"Ada," I say. "A-d-a." The priest can't remember my name, and we have to pay him for the honor of marrying us! Then. Out comes this ring that looks like it came out of a Cracker Jack box. I don't like it, but I put the damn thing on anyway, only it doesn't fit. It's too tight. Which reminds me of the saying: The way you get married shows how your life together as man and wife is going to be. A tight fit, I think.

I can barely get the ring on, but I finally do, and then it's time for the I do's.

I can hardly hear Hector, he sounds like he's about thirteen years old. We "I do" at the same time, and then we laugh and then we "I do" again at the same time. Everyone in the church starts laughing, and I get embarrassed. Then Hector forgets to lift up the veil when he goes to kiss me. More laughter. La Virgie steps in to lift it up, and Hector misses my mouth, so I grab him and cheers break out. Now he's embarrassed and we walk down the aisle: man, wife, and baby. Mr.

Dosamantes' wheelchair is finally out of the way. Everyone stands up and we go outside where they throw birdseed.

"Birdseed? What happened to the rice, Soveida? I always wanted rice!"

"Rice isn't good for the birds, Ada. They say it's better to have birdseed. The birds choke on the rice."

"Shit! This is my wedding and I wanted rice."

"Forget it babes, we're having rice at the reception," says Hector.

"That's Spanish rice, Hector, not the kind of rice I'm talking about. I wanted Uncle Ben's converted rice."

"Sorry, Ada," says Soveida.

And I say, "Whose damn wedding is this, anyway?"

After we got outside, I noticed the wind had come up. I forgot about the tornado watch. The sky did look a little darker, this was about three o'clock, but it still seemed all right. After kissing and hugging ten thousand of Hector's relatives I didn't know, we went to Rogelio's Fine Photography to take pictures. The wedding party was there, which was me, Hector, the Best Man, El Gonie, and the

Maid of Honor, La Virgie. Everyone got mad at me for picking her as Maid of Honor. (Dolly, Soveida, and the old grandma did, anyway.) But like I say, whose wedding is this? Everybody seems to keep forgetting.

La Virgie's no Maid of Honor. She's got five kids and no husband, but she's my friend. Or she was my friend. I didn't know her too good, but Hector and I used to go out with her and El Gonie a lot. The Maid of Honor was between her and Soveida. I probably shoulda picked Soveida. La Virgie was the reason Soveida got divorced from her first husband. Oh well. If I'd known what was going to happen at the reception, I never woulda picked La Virgie Lozano as my Maid of Honor. She doesn't have no Honor. And she's certainly no Maid. She's a tramp, but I didn't know that until about ten p.m. that night in the parking lot of the Knights of Columbus Hall.

Just ask me what could go wrong at the wedding reception, and I'll tell you nothing went right; although for all the things that went wrong, one thing did go right. But I'll tell you about that later. First off, we get into the Knights of Columbus Hall and I notice there's litter all over the outside.

Turns out the janitor didn't clean up like he was supposed to. There's bingo cards all over the folding tables. Hector groans when he sees his cousin, M.J., at the guest book. He never liked her. I'm not exactly sure why he hates most of his relatives. I'll have time to find that out after the wedding. What I really want to know about is his cousin Mara, the one everyone always talks about in a whisper. Soveida invited her to the wedding, but she decided not to come.

"Shit!" Hector whispers loudly. "Tía Adelaida's serving punch." I turn to look at this half-man half-woman serving the sherbert punch. I never wanted sherbert punch, but what can you do? The bride is the last person to know anything.

"Who is she?" I say.

"Mi tía Adelaida. My mom's aunt. She's been paralyzed for fifty years."

"Speaking of paralyzed," I said, "who brought your dad to the church?"

"My mom and her boyfriend, Reldon! Can you believe that!"

"That's nice."

"Nice! What are you, crazy? My grandmother isn't speaking to my mom now."

"Who's that waving to you, Hector?"
"Shit! It's A.J. My first cousin. He's a fag."
"He wants to take a picture. Smile."
"Up his ass! Or maybe I should say up his nose!"

Things went from okay to not so okay to kinda strange to really awful to the real bitching pits.

Of course, Hector got drunk, but not before El Gonie, who was serving champagne and who brought several kegs of beer at the last moment.

Mr. Dosamantes even got drunk! They say that paralyzed people get drunk faster than normal people. He's not really totally paralyzed, just kinda drooly and saggy on the left side. Soveida says he should get better. Someone left Mr. D. in his wheelchair next to the champagne punch, and he kept refilling his little paper cup from the little spouty fountains that came out of the side and splashed on the dry ice. Dolly got mad at him; they had a fight, but her boyfriend, Reldon, broke it up. They were fighting about him getting drunk and then asking Mamá Lupita's maid, Tere, to take him to the bathroom. Dolly got mad at that because she said he shouldn't be asking no pretty young girls to take him to the bathroom. And he started screaming at her that fine, he would just wet his pants then and there. "*I'll* take you to the bathroom," Dolly says. And Mr. D. says, "No way, we're divorced."

Reldon didn't seem to like that idea anyway, and so he volunteers to take Mr. D. to pee. The rest of the night Lupita starts to like Reldon. Which makes Mr. D. pissed. So Mr. D. starts in fighting with his ex-Mrs. D. And she yells at him about how she doesn't like the way he looks at Tere; and he says, "Well look at the way your son is looking at her and she's looking at him." But that makes Dolly even madder. And it even starts to bother me. Everyone is drunk by now. Mr. D. is fighting with his ex-Mrs. D., but we forgot about them when El Gonie and La Virgie started dancing all sexy on the dance floor like they were going to make love out there.

About that time Lupita stepped up to the microphone and introduced *tío* somebody, who read a long poem in Spanish that he said he composed for the wedding. Then someone named El Bluey—it turned out to be Hector's *tío* Bluey, his *tía* Pina's husband—led the wedding marcha around the room. That was the fun part of the wedding. All night people kept pinning dollar bills on my dress. Each dollar bill gives you a chance to dance with either the bride or the groom. My dress was full of pins and dollar bills and so was Hector's suit.

Suddenly, after the marcha I started feeling queasy so I went to the bathroom. A bunch of teenage girls were in there smoking, and the smell got me to feeling worse. I'd eaten the tamales, the macaroni salad, the beans and chile, and the jello salad already, and I'd had at least five champagnes and two beers. I don't know if it was the jumping around during the marcha, going under the London bridge with my head all bent down, snaking around the room with the little hop, or the baby, but I threw up in there for awhile. When I came out, I couldn't find Hector. Neither could Soveida nor anyone else. I danced with a viejito, somebody from Rincón, who had bad breath, which made me queasy again. That made me go back into the bathroom where the girls were still smoking. When I came out, I decided to go outside and get some fresh air and see if the tornado was coming our way after all.

That's when I got the surprise I wasn't expecting. The wind had picked up. With the parking lot lights I could see the open door of Hector's Bonneville, which La Virgie decorated with pink and blue Kleenex flowers. I decided to go over there to close the door. Who do I see inside but La Virgie, her Maid-of-Honor top down to her waist, and there's Hector inside the back seat sucking on one of her chi chis. Well I got sick all over Hector's tux legs, but not before I pulled him out of the back seat and hit him like I never hit anybody before in my life. He kept saying, "Babes, Baby, baby, babes . . ." the way he does, and I let him have it good in between babes. I was yelling and screaming and El Gonie and Soveida came out. El Gonie took that puta home, and I said, "I never want to see you again, you slut. I shoulda picked Soveida as my Maid of Honor!" And you know what the little puta bitch did? She laughed her little puta bitch laugh. And then she walked off like she had espinas, little stickers up her little puta bitch ass.

Soveida pulled me back into the car and settled me down. Not that many people knew what had gone on. Not that night anyway. Soveida didn't want her mother or grandmother to know. I said they should know their little baby boy is a pinche cabrón. And Soveida said, I think they already know that. I stopped screaming and went back inside to the bathroom with Soveida. I had had it. I started screaming at the teenagers: "Get the hell out of here you little shits, go smoke outside!" Whose wedding is this, anyway? All that smoke was giving me the asco bad. I stayed in the bathroom for a good half hour sitting on top of a toilet with my dress all bunched up on my lap. Finally Hector comes in, scaring an old lady who was pulling down her slip, and I start yelling again.

Finally the pendejo convinced me that we'd talk about it later at the Motel 6. We'd planned on staying at the Hilton or maybe La Quinta, but there was a poodle convention in town and there weren't many rooms left.

"This is a wedding, Ada, not a funeral. No one wants to see us fighting."

"I'm not convinced, Hector. You've twisted around my head, I'm not sure any more."

Soveida came in and said that I could figure everything out tomorrow and that she supported me and I could move in with her until I figured out what I wanted to do. Then a gigantic light bulb exploded in my head and I said, "I'm married and I'm going to have a baby!"

I started crying; Hector started crying and said:

"We won't call him Hector Jr., Ada, if that's what you want. We'll call him whatever you want, babes."

"I can? Do you mean that, Hector?"

That kind of softened me up, and he promised he'd never see La Virgie ever again, that she was out of his life, that it was her fault, the whole thing. He explained it to me:

"When you went to the bathroom, La Virgie pinned a five-dollar bill near my cómo se llama and said dance with me. The band played 'Leila,' and after that we were both so hot from dancing that she suggested we go outside to get some fresh air. I decided to get a pack of cigarettes from the glove compartment. I opened up the car and that's when she got in. Suddenly she unzipped her top and there she was in a strapless bra that she pulled down. I yelled to her that someone might see her. When I got in the back seat to cover her up with my tux jacket, she shoved her nipple in my face."

"So why was she saying in a soft voice, put it in, put it in . . ."

"She meant the nipple. A la V, Ada!"

"Oh yeah? Well, I'm not so sure. Don't you a la V me!"

We went around and around until Soveida says, "You two get out of this bathroom. People are asking about you. Someone is giving you a toast."

I hugged Soveida and said, "Thank you, girl." I knew it was hard for her seeing Ivan there with his latest girlfriend. And she says, "I'm healed." Hector invited him. Not me. Even though Soveida says she's recovered from the man, I still feel she loves him the way you love red chile even though it burns you up inside and gives you the hot runs.

Finally I said what the hell and came out of the bathroom with Hector. The band was playing a sweetheart tune and everyone sees us and starts cheering. The *tía* with the mustache grabs my arm. She's got a grip like a truck driver. She starts crying and says "¡Que Díos los bendiga!"

Yeah, sure. But we dance like nothing is wrong, and I keep softening toward the cabrón each circle around the damn K of C Hall.

He grabs me close and whispers: "Let's go, babes!"

"Don't you babes me no more, cabrón! I'll go with you,

but tomorrow I'm filing for divorce."

We smile at his primo the fag and at the *tía* with the strong arms and the mustache, who waves to me across the room still crying, and then we get our things as everyone starts cheering again and whispering and laughing and El Gonie jabs Hector and smiles dirty and then starts up with: "I know what you're going to do."

"Don't count on it, Gonie," I say.

We leave the K of C Hall and drive to the Motel 6. I turn on the television and watch some commercial for something that gets rid of acne. I get so bored I go through Hector's wallet and get his MasterCard and order two tubes of acne creme. Hector's a long time in the bathroom. Good. Stay there. But he comes out naked and smelling of Canoe aftershave and I just turn up the volume on the TV.

"Aren't you going to give me my rights?"

"Suffer, babes," I said. "You already had your rights and your wrongs. I don't want to talk about it now. I need to think about everything. So leave me alone."

Hector falls asleep on the other double bed in the room, and I stay up to watch "The Bug." I don't get the ending when the scientist goes crazy. He falls into the big pit as the fire bugs get in his hair and burn his clothing. I don't get what happened, but then I missed the beginning. What was really cool was when the bugs spelled out the guy's name on the wall. Maybe if there's cucarachas here they'll come out in the middle of the night and spell out something for me. D-I-V-O-R-C-E. I try to forget it's my wedding night.

I wake up real early with Hector in the bed with me and he's warm and I lay there until I can't stand it no longer as he moves closer and says to me the usual, "Come on babes, come on."

I melt like he knows I will and we make love, except I won't turn around to look at him. It's okay this way and he holds me and rocks me back and forth and I cry to myself, and I think: I'm married. I'm really married. And I'm having a baby. Then the bug movie flashes to me, and I think I see the words STUPID PENDEJA on the wall.

The one good thing that came out of the whole stupid thing is that now I don't have to call the baby Hector Jr. if I don't want. I never liked kids called Ray Jr., or Sal Jr., or Ben Jr. Let the kid be himself, I think. I really do hope the baby is a girl. If it is, then I will call her Nereid. The name of some kind of spirit that I read about in junior high English class. Nereids were these beautiful spirits. The name just kind of stuck with me all these years. Just let Hector try and change my mind about this.

That's if the baby's a girl.

If the baby's a boy, I'm going to call him Michael John. I'm not calling him that for Hector or nobody. I'm calling him that just for me. The way I call myself Ada. Not Narada. Not Nada. Ada.

Letters on Love

RAINER MARIA RILKE

There is scarcely anything more difficult than to love one another. That it is work, day labor, day labor, God knows there is no other word for it. And look, added to this is the fact that young people are not prepared for such difficult loving; for convention has tried to make this most complicated and ultimate relationship into something easy and frivolous, has given it the appearance of everyone's being able to do it. It is not so. Love is something difficult and it is more difficult than other things because in other conflicts nature herself enjoins men to collect themselves, to take themselves firmly in hand with all their strength, while in the heightening of love the impulse is to give oneself wholly away. But just think, can that be anything beautiful, to give oneself away not as something whole and ordered, but haphazard rather, bit by bit, as it comes? Can such giving away, that looks so like throwing away and dismemberment, be anything good, can it be happiness, joy, progress? No, it cannot. . . . When you give someone flowers, you arrange them beforehand, don't you? But young people who love each other fling themselves to each other in the impatience and haste of their passion, and they don't notice at all what a lack of mutual esteem lies in this disordered giving of themselves; they notice it with astonishment and indignation only from the dissension that arises between them out of all this disorder. And once there is disunity between them, the confusion grows with every day; neither of the two has anything unbroken, pure, and unspoiled about him any longer, and amid the disconsolateness of a break they try to hold fast to the semblance of their happiness (for all that was really supposed to be for the sake of happiness). Alas, they are scarcely able to recall any more what they meant by happiness. In his uncertainty each becomes more and more unjust toward the other; they who wanted to do each other good are now handling one another in an imperious and intolerant manner, and in the struggle somehow to get out of their untenable and unbearable state of confusion, they commit the greatest fault that can happen to human relationships: they become impatient. They hurry to a conclusion; to come, as they believe, to a final decision, they try once and for all to establish their relationship, whose surprising changes have frightened them, in order to remain the same now and *forever* (as they say). That is only the last error in this long chain of errings linked fast to one another. What is dead cannot even be clung to (for it crumbles and changes its character); how much less can what is living and alive be treated definitively, once and for all. Self-transformation is precisely what life is, and human relationships, which are an extract of life, are the most changeable of all, rising and falling from minute to minute, and lovers are those in whose relationship and contact no one moment resembles another. People between whom nothing accustomed, nothing that has already been present before ever takes place, but many new, unexpected, unprecedented things. There are such relationships which must be a very great, almost unbearable happiness, but they can occur only between very rich natures and between those who, each for himself, are richly ordered and composed; they can unite only two wide, deep, individual worlds.—Young people—it is obvious—cannot achieve such a relationship, but they can, if they understand their life properly, grow up slowly to such happiness and prepare themselves for it. They must not forget, when they love, that they are beginners, bunglers of life, apprentices in love,—must *learn* love, and that (like *all* learning) wants peace, patience, and composure!

The Omen

OVID

Out upon it and alack!
Here's a nasty blow.
She has sent my letter back
Scrawled across it —"No."
What a cruel word to bring,
Devil take the horrid thing.

Well, another time I'll know,
when I deal with women,
I had better credence show
To an adverse omen.
When I gave the note to Nell
She tripped her foot and almost fell.

If I write another day,
Prithee, Nell, beware;

When you go upon your way
Walk with sober care.
Then, it may be, I shall find
That my lady is more kind.

The Different Stars

W. S. MERWIN

I could never have come to the present without you
remember that
from whatever stage we may again
watch it appear

with its lines clear
pain
having gone from there

so that we may well wonder
looking back on us here what tormented us
what great difficulty invisible
in a time that by then looks simple
and is irrevocable

pain having come from there

my love
I tend to think of division as the only evil
when perhaps it is merely my own

that unties
one day the veins one the arteries
that prizes less
as it receives than as it loses
that breaks the compasses
cannot be led or followed
cannot choose what to carry
into grief
even
unbinds will unbinds
our hands
pages of the same story

what is it
they say can turn even this into wisdom
and what is wisdom if it is not
now

in the loss that has not left this place

oh if we knew
if we knew what we needed if we even knew
the stars would look to us to guide them

Gather Together in My Name

MAYA ANGELOU

Love was what I had been waiting for. I had done grown-up things out of childish ignorance or juvenile bravado, but now I began to mature. I became pleased with my body because it gave me such pleasure. I shopped for myself carefully for the first time. Searching painstakingly for just the right clothes instead of buying the first thing off the rack. Unfortunately my taste was as new as my interest. Once when Curly was to take me out to dinner, I bought a smart yellow crepe dress with black roses, black baby-doll shoes, whose straps sank a full inch into my ankles, and an unflattering wide coolie hat with veil. I pinned a small cluster of yellow rose buds on my bosom and was ready for the fray.

He only asked me to remove the corsage.

Curly had said at the beginning of our affair that he had a girl who worked in a San Diego shipyard and her job would be up soon. Then they'd go back to New Orleans and get married. I hastily stored the information in that inaccessible region of the mind where one puts the memory of pain and other unpleasantries. For the while it needn't bother me, and it didn't.

He was getting out of the Navy and only had a couple of months before all his papers would be cleared. Southern upbringing and the terror of war made him seem much older than his thirty-one years.

We took my son for long walks through parks; when people complimented us on our child, he played the proud papa and accepted. At playland on the beach we road the Ferris wheel and loop-the-loop and gooed ourselves with salt-water taffy. Late afternoons we took the baby back to the sitter and then went to his hotel and one more, or two more or three more love parties. I never wanted it to end. I bought things for him. A watch (he already had one), a sports coat (too small), another ring, and I paid for them myself. I couldn't hear his protestations. I wasn't buying things. I was buying time.

One day after work he took me to the sitter's. He sat and held the baby. His silence should have told me something. Maybe it did, but again I didn't want to know. We left in a quiet mood. He only said, "I want me a boy like that. Just like that."

Since we weren't heading for the hotel, I asked where we were going.

"I'm taking you to your house."

"Why?"

No answer.

He found a parking space a half-block away. The streetlights were just coming on and a soft fog dimmed the world. He reached in the back seat and took out two large boxes. He handed them to me and said, "Give me a kiss."

I tried to laugh, to pretend that the kiss was payment for the gifts, but the laugh lied. He kissed me lightly and looked at me long.

"Reet. My girl friend is here and I'll be checking out of the hotel tonight."

I didn't cry because I couldn't think.

"You're going to make some man a wonderful wife. I mean it. These things are for you and the baby. I hate to say good-bye, but I gotta."

He probably said more, but all I remember is walking from the car to my front door. Trying for my life's sake to control the angry lurchings of my stomach. Trying to walk upright carrying the awkward boxes. I had to set down the boxes to find the door key, and habit fitted it into the lock. I entered the hall without hearing him start the car.

Because he had not lied, I was forbidden anger. Because he had patiently and tenderly taught me love, I could not use hate to erase the pain. I had to bear it.

I am certain, with the passage of time, that he loved me. Maybe for the loveless waif I was. Maybe he felt pity for the young mother and fatherless child, and so decided to give us what we both needed for two months. I don't know. I'm only certain that for some reason he loved me and that he was a good man.

The loss of young first love is so painful that it borders on the ludicrous.

I even embarrassed myself. Weeks after Charles left, I stumbled around San Francisco operating in the familiar. The lovely city disappeared in my fog. Nothing I did to food made it interesting to me. Music became a particular aggravation, for every emotional lyric had obviously been written for me alone.

> Gonna take a sentimental journey
> gonna set my heart at ease . . .

Charles had taken that journey and left me all alone. I was one emotional runny sore. To be buffeted about emotionally was not new, only the intensity and reason were. The new pain and discomfort was physical. My body had been awakened and fed, and suddenly I discovered I had a ravenous appetite. My natural reticence and habit of restraint prevented me from seeking other satisfaction even if it could be found.

I began to lose weight, which, with my height and thinness, I could ill afford to do. The burst of energy which had propelled me into beauty salons and dress shops was now as absent as my gone lover. I longed and pined, sighed and yearned, cried and generally slouched around feeling dismal and bereaved. By eighteen I managed to look run down if not actually run over.

My brother Bailey again was my savior, a role he fulfilled most of my early years.

He returned to the city after some months on an ammunition ship, and came to the restaurant to see me.

"My. What the hell's happened to you?" The way I looked seemed to anger rather than worry him. I introduced him to my employer. She said, "Your brother. He awful little, ain't he? I mean, to be your brother?"

Bailey thanked her smoothly, allowing just the tail of his sarcasm to flick in her face. She never noticed.

"I said, what's the matter with you? Have you been sick?" I held in the tears that wanted to pour into my brother's hands.

"No. I'm okay."

I thought at the time that it was noble to bear the ills one had silently. But not so silently that others didn't know one was bearing them.

"What time do you get off?"

"One o'clock. I'm off tomorrow, so I'm going out to get the baby."

"I'll be back and take you. Then we can talk."

He turned to Mrs. Dupree. "And a good day to you, too, madam." Bailey did little things with such a flourish. He might have been the Count of Monte Cristo, or Cyrano saying farewell to fair Roxanne.

After he had gone, Mrs. Dupree grinned her lips into a pucker. "He's as cute as a little bug."

I busied myself amid the pots. If she thought likening my big brother to an insect would please me, she had another think coming.

The baby crawled around the floor of my room as I told Bailey of my great love affair. Of the pain of discovery of pain. He nodded understanding and said nothing.

I thought that while I had his attention I might as well throw in my other sadness. I told him that because my old schoolmates laughed at me, I felt more isolated than I had in Stamps, Arkansas.

He said, "He sounds like a nice guy" and "I think it's time for you to leave San Francisco. You could try Los Angeles or San Diego."

"But I don't know where I'd live. Or get a job." Although

I was miserable in San Francisco, the idea of another place frightened me. I thought of Los Angeles and it was a gray vast sea without ship or lighthouse.

"I can't just tear Gus away. He's used to the woman who looks after him."

"But she's not his mother."

"I've got a good job here."

"But surely you don't mean to make cooking Creole food your life's work."

I hadn't thought about it. "I have a nice room here. Don't you think it's nice?"

He looked at me squarely, forcing me to face my fears. "Now, My, if you're happy being miserable, enjoy it, but don't ask me to feel sorry for you. Just get all down in it and wallow around. Take your time to savor all its subtleties, but don't come to me expecting sympathy."

He knew me too well. It was true. I was loving the role of the jilted lover. Deserted, yet carrying on. I saw myself as the heroine, solitary, standing under a streetlight's soft yellow glow. Waiting. Waiting. As the fog comes in, a gentle rain falls but doesn't drench her. It is just enough to make her shiver in her white raincoat (collar turned up). Oh, he knew me too well.

"If you want to stay around here looking like death eating a soda cracker, that's your business. There are some rights no one has the right to take from you. That's one. Now, what do you want to do?"

That evening I decided to go to Los Angeles. At first I thought I'd work another month, saving every possible penny. But Bailey said, "When you make up your mind to make a change you have to follow through on the wave of decision." He promised me two hundred dollars when his ship paid off and suggested I tell my boss that I'd be leaving in a week.

I had never had two hundred dollars of my own. It sounded like enough to live on for a year.

The prospect of a trip to Los Angeles returned my youth to me.

My mother heard my plans without surprise. "You're a woman. You can make up your own mind." She hadn't the slightest idea that not only was I not a woman, but what passed for my mind was animal instinct. Like a tree or a river, I merely responded to the winds and the tides.

She might have seen that, but her own mind was misted with the knowledge of a failing marriage, and the slipping away of the huge sums of money which she had enjoyed and thought her due. Her fingers still glittered with diamonds and she was a weekly customer at the most expensive shoe store in town, but her pretty face had lost its carefree adornment and her smile no longer made me think of day breaking.

"Be the best of anything you get into. If you want to be a whore, it's your life. Be a damn good one. Don't chippy at anything. Anything worth having is worth working for."

It was her version of Polonius' speech to Laertes. With that wisdom in my pouch, I was to go out and buy my future.

about the authors

MAYA ANGELOU, author, poet, playwright, professional stage and screen producer, director, performer, and singer, is the author of such well-known works as *I Know Why the Caged Bird Sings* and *Journey of the Heart*.

ALICE ADAMS was a prolific author of short stories and novels such as *Families and Survivors* and *Medicine Men*. She died in San Francisco in 1999.

RAYMOND CARVER was a prolific short story author and poet whose collections include *Where I'm Calling From* and *What We Talk About When We Talk About Love*.

DENISE CHÁVEZ is an author and playwright from Las Cruces, New Mexico. Her works include *The Last of the Menu Girls* and *Face of an Angel*.

F. SCOTT FITZGERALD is considered to be one of the greatest American authors. His books include *The Great Gatsby* and *Tender Is the Night*.

IVAN KLIMA is a Czech author whose work was banned in Czechoslovakia under the Communist regime, but has remained a well-respected internationally voice in literature throughout his career.

W. S. MERWIN is the Pulitzer Prize winning poet of works such as *The Carrier of Ladders* and *The Poem of the Cid*.

OVID, born in Sulmo, Italy, in 43 B.C., was trained as a lawyer but is best known for the poetry contained in *Art of Love* and *Metamorphoses*.

DR. M. SCOTT PECK is the best-selling author of *The Road Less Traveled*. He lives in northern Connecticut.

RAINER MARIA RILKE was a poet born in Prague in 1875. His *Letters to a Young Poet* is still highly regarded and widely read around the world.

RUMI was a scholar and mystic poet who lived in Afghanistan and Turkey from 1207 to 1273.

BERNHARD SCHLINK was born in Germany in 1944. He is a lawyer and professor, and the author of several prize-winning crime novels.

ANNE SEXTON, Pulitzer Prize–winning poet, lived her whole life in or near Boston until she committed suicide in 1974.

LAOTZU, author and holy man, wrote his seminal work *The Tao Te Ching* in China more than 2,000 years ago. It remains an influential and important work to this day.

JEANETTE WINTERSON, a British author who lives in London, is the prize-winning author of *The Passion*, *Written on the Body*, and *Sexing the Cherry*.